A

Search For Divine Truth

Masonic Learning Centers for Dyslexic Children
will be given all proceeds received by the author,
or his estate, from the sale of *Hurry Up Son.*

by

Kenton E. McElhattan

To: Arnold J. Sholder, M.D.
May you enjoy some thoughts
written by a "3M" patient of yours,
who is forever grateful for saving
his life from prostate cancer.
Kenton E. McElhattan
December 22, 2008
Happy Hanukkah!

DORRANCE PUBLISHING CO., INC.
PITTSBURGH, PENNSYLVANIA 15222

ISBN # 0-8059-6241-7

Printed in the United States of America

First Printing
For information or to order additional books, please write:
Dorrance Publishing Co., Inc.
701 Smithfield Street
Pittsburgh, Pennsylvania 15222
U.S.A.
1-800-788-7654
Or visit our web site and on-line catalog at
www.dorrancepublishing.com

FOREWORD

Before submitting my first piece for publication to a professional journal, I sent it to a trusted teacher, an often-published seminary professor, for his evaluation. He sent it back with some recommended changes and added this caveat: "To write something for the public domain is the literal equivalent of sticking out one's chin and inviting others to punch it. Only the bravest, or the most foolhardy, will do that because to do so is to set oneself up for denigration. There will always be those who criticize what you write. This is not said to discourage you but to prepare you for what will almost surely come." I still recall his words every time I submit something for publication. However, something else he said became one of the great motivations for my own writing: "What we write may be the only thing by which we are remembered long after we are gone. So, write more and publish often. Your great-grandchildren will appreciate you for it and know you through it."

This book is by a great-grandfather who wants his grandchildren and great-grandchildren to know him and to know about some of his life's experiences and his journey toward God. Its influence, however, needs to spread far beyond one family. His words need to be read by you and your family. That is just one reason I encouraged him to publish this book. K. E. McElhattan is not just one of my parishioners; he is one of my dearest friends, and one of the wisest, most gracious and loving people I know.

As you read his words, you may disagree with—perhaps even challenge—some things he writes. Of this, however, you can be certain: This is a book from the heart of a man who loves God and His Son Jesus. What is more, it is a book by an unusually modest man God has used and continues to use magnificently in ways for which K.E. will take no credit. You will find no puffery in these pages and you will find no stories that try to persuade you of the author's greatness. K.E. is far too modest to allow anything like that to be published.

What you will find is an authentic personality and the plain, unvarnished honesty about how God has drawn K.E. on a search for divine truth. Many who read it will be intrigued to the point that it will be hard to put it down. Others will want to read it in small bite-sized pieces and ponder its message. His story will make you laugh and make you cry. Perhaps it will cause you to think about your own life's journey and your potential to impact the lives of others.

"Ye shall seek me, and find me, when ye shall search for me with all your heart" (Jeremiah 29:13). God, who gave us these words and who is found uniquely in His Son Jesus Christ, has many ways of tapping us on the shoulder. This is how He tapped and tapped again on K. E. McElhattan's shoulder. Read on. You will learn some new things.

Dr. R. Leslie Holmes, Senior Pastor
The First Presbyterian Church of Pittsburgh
320 Sixth Avenue
Pittsburgh, PA 15222

IV

Disclaimer

This is not intended to be an autobiography or a story about our family. Personal references and reference to family members are only made to complete or round out the particular story being written. When others are quoted a diligent effort was made to be as accurate as possible with the quotation and what I believe they meant to convey. It is not possible to verify the actual words spoken or the meaning when people being quoted are deceased.

Like myself, family members have served as Church Trustees, Elders, Deacons, Sunday School Superintendents, Teachers, and have attended Seminary. In all probability they will disagree with some of the *Stories About a Variety of Things*. If that is true then they are urged to keep an open mind and diligently study material in the bibliography and ancient documents that are now available. A mind dedicated to the search for TRUTH! Many documents and especially the Dead Sea Scrolls translations were not available during my years of active participation in church work.

Also, my words are in no way intended to be a satirical writing about Christianity, the Bible, or critical of anyone's beliefs. Discrepancies do exist between what the author was taught as facts and what seeking the truth in later life has revealed.

The teachings of Jesus are just as relevant and important today as they were during the time when Bible authors composed the scriptures. The teachings attributed to Jesus by Bible authors are now known to be the wisdom developed from trial and error by more ancient civilizations. Those civilizations taught the initiates by using the allegorical method, which took several years to attain proficiency. Pythagoras studied in Egypt for many years to achieve teaching proficiency. (See page 40)

Christianity today expects people to become proficient and devout followers by spending only an hour or so on Sunday morning listening to the preacher or teacher. As a former teacher, elder, and Sunday school superintendent it embarrasses me to admit how inadequately trained all of us were to assume such important responsibilities. In fact, we had no training at all and were never given proficiency tests for our teaching ability or knowledge of the subject.

Do not gamble with your salvation by depending on amateurs!

CONTENTS

Dedication

Dedicated to people with inquiring minds who are searching for Divine Truth. People with open minds seeking Truth that can only be revealed by the Grand Architect of the Universe. People with the initiative to use their brain and look beyond the tired and worn clichés such as, ***this is the True Word of God.***

If you seek Truth, you will not seek to gain a victory by every possible means; and when you have found Truth, you need not fear being defeated.
...Epictetus, *CXLIX, Harvard Classics*

****

Comments about the Forward

There have been only two pastors in my entire life that I would describe as magnanimous. Only a magnanimous pastor would permit his name to be associated with any book that contains stories some people might consider controversial, or stories that may conflict with Christian theology, dogma, and creed. Dr. R. Leslie Holmes is one of those pastors.

When the manuscript was completed, I felt an obligation to submit certain parts of it to my pastor. Research had led me to write about items that an ordained minister may not agree with. Since Leslie Holmes is my pastor, I did not want to take him by surprise if by chance he should ever read some of my *Stories About a Variety Of Things.*

The Forward by Leslie Holmes does not mean that he approves everything in this book. The words are all mine. My original intent was to make only a few copies for my grandsons and others to debate, argue about, disagree with, and hopefully inspire them to individually find their Spirituality through searching for Divine Truth.

Dr. R. Leslie Holmes encouraged me to publish the book, because it is an honest admission about my journey to seek Divine Truth. At eleven years of age, our preacher confused me by insisting we have a 'Jesus experience' in the church joining ceremony. Concurrent with that occasion we had an unorthodox Sunday school teacher that taught us to always challenge the mythical Bible stories, and the intent of the preacher by insisting they were 'Gospel Truth.' The preacher and teacher created a lifelong dichotomy for me about the accuracy of Bible stories and other religious documents.

VIII

The teacher was a maverick that loved to have the class get into heated debates about the many inconsistencies in the Bible. (See pages 10 and 13) Between the preacher and the teacher they left that eleven-year-old kid confused. As I get older and give more thought to mortality it makes me realize what a lasting effect that both good and poor role models can have on young people during their impressionable years.

In addition to the mental confusion caused by the preacher and teacher my father, the Sunday school superintendent, told me, *"You are one of those unusual people that will not accept anything but proven facts. You believe nothing unless you can personally prove it to be true. Someday, you may learn there are things that cannot be proven on that drafting table in your room, or with mathematics."* (See page 4) Many times I thought about his words while doing research on items referred to in this book. Most fathers understand sons better than what the son may believe. My father understood me all too well, as I am still seeking to find the truth about items that other people appear to accept just on faith alone, or that the preacher assured them it is gospel truth.

Dr. Holmes understands that some people never experience a sudden religious conversion and that we may learn more by opposition than conformity. By searching for historical truth and writing about it I hope others are challenged to seek the Divine Truth and Spirituality you may not have realized is within you. That has been true for me. Too often we take comfort in assuming that God is a father-type deity, which is reverting to theism, or a daddy that will always look after us. As Dr. Holmes writes, *perhaps I am sticking my chin out and inviting others to punch it.* If any of the stories about a grandfather's search for Divine Truth help you to discover the individual spirituality within your soul then it is worth getting my chin punched!

PREFACE

This book is the result of a visit my daughter and her four sons made to our cottage during the summer of 2001. All four grandsons were college students. Their visit coincided with my studies of attempting to seek Truth. The previous year I had been coroneted a 33° Mason, and assumed an obligation to seek Truth, Righteousness, and Justice. Righteousness and justice are fairly straightforward. During my studies it became obvious that Truth is quite elusive. The *American Heritage Dictionary*, gives many synonyms and definitions. It summarizes, **"*Truth* is a comprehensive term that in all of its nuances *implies accuracy* and *honesty*."**

College students have fertile minds. To further my studies of Truth, our grandsons were engaged in conversations concerning truth and their philosophical beliefs. I had absolutely no idea what the composite beliefs of four college students might be, but anticipated they could teach old granddad a lot. During one memorable evening when we were all together I suggested, *"Let's devote time for each of us to explain what we think Truth actually is and summarize our beliefs and opinions as they relate to life, religion, and the Bible."* My turn was to be last. Without telling them, I did not want to influence their thinking by speaking first. It might make them feel they were obligated to agree with their grandfather. Even grandparents can be wrong! It was especially surprising, even shocking, to learn their opinions about the Bible. One grandson went so far as to say the Bible is just a lot of ancient myths and propaganda that had been canonized through the years by the Roman Catholic Church in order to seek control over the populace.

When it came my turn to speak, my grandsons were told how my life had been influenced as an eleven-year-old boy. At that age in 1933 there were seven students approved to join the church after passing the final test in catechism class. During the evening acceptance ceremony the preacher urged me to 'hurry up son' and find Jesus so I could be saved from my sins, and the church service would not run overtime. Church membership was a prerequisite to be eligible for the Teen Boys Sunday School class of the Knox, PA Methodist Church. Victor Botts taught the class and my father was the Sunday School Superintendent.

My grandsons thought the experience of a preacher trying to save an eleven-year-old kid from his sins was really funny. They also thought it was unusual to have sex education in a boys Sunday school class. We also discussed the possibility that teenagers may not know what they believe with regard to religion.

Following discussions on many items such as WWII, Christian holidays and rituals, Freemasonry, and others, it seemed appropriate that some of my comments should be written down. The discipline of documentation forces me to put some of the things that I said in writing, and should eliminate from future discussions what granddad may or may not have said.

This book consists of stories about a variety of things. Some are facts from my life. Others are conclusions reached after making a diligent effort to find the truth in the Bible stories. Also, people are quoted that have influenced my life and thinking. Doing research that may appear silly to 'Christian believers' can help others to discover what they intuitively believe. Unfortunately, some of us require the more difficult path of opposition, rather than conformity, to arrive at a similar conclusion.

It is not the author's intention to influence or impress anyone. It is an honest effort to document experiences and subjects that have made an impression on me. Throughout the book the written words are no more than a grandfather speaking directly and honestly about a variety of things he has learned. It is difficult to express in words the disappointment in learning that things believed to be the 'gospel truth' most of my life are actually ancient mythical fables, appropriated by the Christian church, canonized, and then taught as the infallible Word of God. After research, it became obvious my one grandson deserved more credit than what he had been given about his comments on the Bible.

If you are one that believes the Christian church should never be questioned or challenged on dogma or creed, and the Bible is a book of facts, then reading this booklet is a complete waste of your time. Unless you do your own open-minded in depth research on subjects discussed then you will probably conclude the author is a bit flaky.

All I can suggest is that voluminous information and historical facts are available to confirm the Christian Church borrowed, and then canonized ancient mythical practices as its dogma and creed. Plagiarism or thievery, not divine intervention may be more appropriate words to describe the action of the Roman Church. However, that in no way diminishes the moral teachings that the church claims to be the Word of God as taught by Jesus. Those teachings were developed long before the Jesus era. They are just as important today for mankind as they were thousands of years prior to the time people attributed the teachings to Jesus.

Scholars are learning that our ancient ancestors were far more developed in their philosophical beliefs (wisdom) than previously thought. Even with current technology we cannot duplicate the machine-shop accuracy used by the Egyptians to finish the stones used to build the pyramids. It is truly exciting to learn how advanced our ancestors were. Their knowledge was documented for posterity and deposited in the library at Alexandria, Egypt. That knowledge was lost forever when the Christian Church destroyed the library and burned the documents.

Reading this book may irritate you or challenge some of your current beliefs if you have never done research or seriously thought about the subjects discussed. Many people go through life believing everything in the Bible is literally true and that every word spoken from their church pulpit is the Word of God, as most preachers say before reading the scripture. They never study the Bible inconsistencies or how at one time every book in the Bible was classed as heretical. Do they know that the Old Testament was taken directly from the Hebrew Scriptures (Jewish Tanak) and then claimed to be theirs by the Christian church? Those were certainly my general beliefs prior to the occurrence of two things. One was an obligation to seek the Truth. The other was listening to what my grandson's were saying and then do further research.

Others may reach different conclusions after studying the information used in my continuing search for Truth. My conclusions cannot all be documented, because the more I search for Truth the more I realize that seeking Truth is a lifetime learning experience. No theologian has been able to give satisfactory answers to my many questions. A stalemate is reached when I am told that Biblical fantasies and church dogma and creed cannot be questioned. They must be accepted on blind faith, which means you cannot use your God-given brain.

Attempting to define God through the limitations of human language is an exercise in frustration. Mankind has been attempting to do just that since our ancient ancestors appeared on earth. Trying to learn about God in the Bible results in a deity that evolves as mankind progresses. A God that changes according to the situation, and is defined in the male gender, is obviously the writing of humans attempting to explain a deity according to the beliefs during the period of time in which they lived.

Hebrew Scriptures, now the Christian Old Testament, were written during a male dominated society so they described God in male terms. Women were treated as a commodity during that period of time. The Hebrew God, later adopted by the Christians, was intended to be feared. He was described as war loving, murderous, and even gave orders to, *slay old men outright, young men and maidens, little children and women.* (Ezekiel 9: 4-6) Is that the type of God we should worship? My personal belief is that God is so much more than the crude Biblical descriptions. Limitations are placed on God by even trying to define a deity in human terms. Wouldn't an ape define God in terms of an ape?

Nearly seven thousand years ago, the Egyptians described their god as being for all people, male and female, that was not an ethnic god like the god that was later described in Hebrew Scriptures. Following are quotes from Egyptian writings that document what their God said thousands of years before Judaism and Christianity:

"*I united myself to my shadow, and I sent forth Shu and Tefnut out of myself; thus being one God I became three. I, the evolver of evolutions evolved myself. I laid the foundations of all things by my will, and all things evolved themselves therefrom.*" "*God is Truth and He liveth by Truth and He feedeth thereon. God is hidden and no man knoweth His form. He is a mystery unto His creatures. God is life and through Him only man liveth. God is father and mother, the father of fathers and the mother of mothers.*"

The first sentence quoted above appears to negate that a Trinity is unique to Christianity as taught by Christian denominations. Also, God in the Papyrus is defined as both male and female, which is more acceptable to many people than the patriarchal Hebrew God (now Christian) that is described as being male only—a father type image, or theism. (See page 111)

Studying ancient Egyptian hieroglyphics is a fascinating exercise for an engineer that enjoys working with symbols and characters that metaphorically condense information that would otherwise require much explanation. What confused me in hieroglyphics was that many of them represent a similar meaning in Christianity. The problem it created was; '*How could any hieroglyphic have a similar meaning in Christianity, when the hieroglyphic could not be transliterated until after 1799 when the Rosetta stone was discovered in the Nile River Delta? There has to be a relationship.*'

After a lot of searching, I concluded it must have been Moses. Although the heredity of Moses was an ethnic Jew, he was adopted by the Pharaoh's daughter and raised as an Egyptian. In Acts 7:22 it states, '*Moses was instructed in all the wisdom of the Egyptians, and was mighty in words and deeds.*' If that Biblical sentence is true then Moses would have been fluent in Egyptian hieroglyphics and other knowledge. When Moses assumed leadership of the Jewish people, after age forty, the message those hieroglyphics conveyed would carryover into the Hebrew Scriptures, and later into Christianity, although the ability to read them was lost. The remarkable similarities between Egyptian hieroglyphics and their later meaning in Christianity would make an interesting book. For the sake of brevity, I will refer to only two and hope they might be interesting enough for you to do your own research on others:

1. ✝–This is the Egyptian hieroglyphic for the word '*Savior.*' You must admit it would make a fascinating story to trace this symbol from the

Egyptian language to the symbol of the Latin cross for Christianity that was adopted at the Nicene Convention nearly 300 years after the death of Jesus.

2. *Amen*–The Egyptian hieroglyphic for the name *Amen*, creator god of Thebes, is identical to the mitre worn by the Pope and current-day bishops on their head. It has a split front and rear section and includes a tail. Christians adopted the word 'amen' from Judaism where it also meant, *"let it be so"* following a prayer. Are both Christians and Jews unknowingly paying homage to the original god Amen of Thebes when they say his name following a prayer? Are we asking for a blessing from the god Amen that our prayer requests may become true? When you see the Pope or a bishop you might ask, why he is symbolically wearing *Amen* on his head? I do not know!

Attending church is usually enjoyable–otherwise why attend? Music, fellowship, and sermons that teach morality are inspiring. However, during the week that follows some people act like they learned nothing from the sermon. The pastor should not be criticized for that. Only through God can a spiritual experience be created that will sustain you during the highs and lows of a secular life. It is like a farmer saying, 'I can lead my horse to water, but I can't make him drink.' Pastors work hard preparing sermons and attempt to lead, but they cannot make you drink. Spirituality comes from within!

Working at my tree farm provides a more intense spiritual renewal for me than attending a church service. Communing with Nature (God) truly revitalizes the soul. A healing process is experienced that cannot be explained, nor can it be achieved from any other source. Seedlings struggle to grow, beavers cut trees, squirrels steal nuts, weeds grow tenaciously, deer browse on seedlings, fruit blossoms freeze, beetles eat leaves, and many other problems at a tree farm are downright frustrating. However, when you relax and sit down to enjoy the sunset, and reflect upon all of the complicated relationships within Nature, there is a renewing of the soul from an inner-voice. The Grand Architect of the universe seems to be telling me to:

"Slow down son. Use your brain! You call MY divine creations problems. You may be the problem! Perhaps the weeds and bugs do not like being killed by chemical sprays. You have a larger brain, but you will never know all of the fundamental truths about other forms of life. Levels of thought exist that your Creator will never permit any person to penetrate while in the human form of life. Communing with Nature will teach you some truths. My gifts to you were freedom of choice and a brain to use. Your salvation will depend upon the choices made during the time you live on earth. You are encouraged to seek fundamental truths, which can lead you to discover that Divine Truth, and Spirituality, will be found only within your soul."

Hurry Up Son!

but,
"Leave Your Brains in the Parking Lot."

Stories About a Variety of Things

HURRY UP SON

"Leave Your Brain in the Parking Lot!"

"Hurry up son. You're delaying the service. The others professed they found Jesus tonight and have gone back to their seats." Mrs. McCaskey whispered those words to Kenton McElhattan while he knelt at the altar of the Methodist Church in Knox, PA. The year was 1933[1]. The occasion was an evening church service. Reverend Charles W. McCaskey wanted to show-off his new Catechism Class graduates and have them accepted as new church members.

Seven boys and girls had faithfully attended the catechism classes for four weeks in preparation to become new church members. The catechism course was held on Saturdays and several evenings. Curriculum consisted of learning about the mysteries of Jesus Christ, the disciples, church law, and memorizing the Apostles' Creed, Ten Commandments, and the Beatitudes. Students' ages were eleven to fourteen years.

The build-up and excitement of attending catechism classes to be eligible for admission into membership of the Methodist Church mysteries and Christianity was an exciting time. It acted somewhat as a mental bridge between the time when we had finally realized Santa Claus was a total myth, and the time we arrived at puberty. We were taught what the personal benefits would be after confessing our sins and joining the church. At that age, the only sin I could think of was harassing three sisters.

That was the time when I learned it is fun to sin. The preacher taught us that brothers and sisters should love one another just like all of God's family. To disagree or argue within a family he said was a sin. Perhaps he was only trying to make a point, but we took him literally. It seemed odd the preacher thought it was a sin for kids to pick on each other. We all knew adults in God's family at the Methodist Church who wouldn't even speak and hated one another. It took brains to choose the proper time for the sin of harassing sisters. Discretion was also required because parents could not be present.

Earlier in the evening church service, Reverend McCaskey had called groups of people to the alter where they could confess their sins and go back to the seats assured that Jesus Christ had forgiven them. We had never seen this fellow Jesus Christ, but were assured beyond any doubt that He was present with us. The preacher repeatedly said that Jesus was there with us

---

[1] Catechism Certificate April 16, 1933.

during all of the class periods, but He eluded most of us.

The Communicant Class was called to the altar last. It was Reverend McCaskey's highlight of the evening. His glowing remarks about our performance and character really made me wonder if I should be present. He said the class would kneel at the altar and individually receive Jesus Christ as their savior while his wife helped. Everyone was assured they would have the experience of Jesus entering into their life. We were told that when the class returned to their seats they would be new people with the spirit of Jesus Christ within them. Boy! I thought this is really going to be a big deal. I'm going to be someone different when it is over. Maybe this will even be more fun than teasing sisters.

While kneeling at the altar with our eyes closed as instructed the McCaskeys took turns placing their hands on our heads and saying, "You are now receiving the spirit of Jesus." On the second round they asked if we had experienced the sensation of receiving Jesus Christ into our life. "Do you feel the glow and warmth of His presence?" We were asked to whisper to them that we did. As each student whispered they had received Him and felt His presence they were instructed to return to their pew seat and told, "you now have the spirit of Jesus Christ within you."

Jack Hiwiller whispered loud enough that we overheard heard him tell the preacher, "Lord I am saved. Jesus just told me that I should become a preacher." Jack was later billed in surrounding towns as the Boy Preacher and gave sermons in church services. He became a real hotshot with the girls. Reverend McCaskey treated him as a very special discovery. Even the Franklin Gospel Tabernacle in Franklin, PA was blessed to have Jack preach there several times along with Billy Sunday. His preaching days ended at fourteen years of age. We never knew why. Most of us thought he was preaching about things that he did not understand, because we didn't. Being the Boy Preacher had somewhat ostracized Jack from being one of the 'rough and tumble' gang in town. Perhaps he came to the conclusion it was more important to be accepted by your peers than to preach about something you really did not understand. Unfortunately, Jack was killed in an automobile accident a few years later that made all of us feel terrible about losing him.

Ronald Gross, another member of the class, became a short-term teen-age lay minister under the guidance of the McCaskeys. Ron's preaching career ended abruptly when he ran away from home before reaching age sixteen. It was an awful worry for his parents not to know where he was for several years. He surfaced in Hawaii as a member of the armed services about a year before the December 7, 1941, bombing of Pearl Harbor. On Ron's first trip home his preaching was limited to the fellows in town that loafed at the three gasoline service stations. The sermon was usually about how wonderful it was to have sex with those beautiful dark-skinned Hawaiian girls. Most of us failed to appreciate his sermons, because we hadn't even been out of town. Later, Ron had some personal problems that the other fellows did not understand. In later life, some of us wondered if Reverend McCaskey might have over-promoted the Boy Preacher idea so that he would get more recognition in the synod by the boys being in his congregation.

When Reverend McCaskey got to me that night and asked what I had seen and felt he was obviously very disappointed. Perhaps I shouldn't have told him the truth. All I could see was darkness with my eyes closed and my knees were getting sore from kneeling. He whispered, "You are the last one at the altar. I'll send my wife over to work with you," and made some comment about my brain that I didn't quite catch. I think he said something about leaving my brain in my father's car in the parking lot. That would not have been possible because we had walked to church. Mrs. McCaskey again whispered about me delaying the service and to hurry up. She was then told a 'white-lie' that I had experienced Jesus and felt the warmth of his presence. Actually, my knees were sore and I hadn't seen or felt a thing except the preacher's cold hand on my head. She congratulated me and said, "return to the pew seat as you are now saved. Jesus Christ will always be with you."

Saved from what? I have always wondered, what were we supposed to be saved from? Was it teasing sisters or some other horrible sin? How could Jesus Christ always be with an eleven-year-old boy when He was supposedly killed a couple thousand years ago? Where was He when a German at La Petit, France killed my uncle, Oren Berlin, in 1918? Did Jesus Christ think more of that German soldier than He did of my mother's brother, a nineteen-year-old American soldier in Company F of the 112th Infantry? Why did my younger brother, Donald, die at age 2 years 9 months of whooping cough and intestinal flu? If Jesus Christ could save two crazies by transferring their demons to a herd of pigs that ran to the sea and drowned,[1] why couldn't He save my brother? Did the owner of those drowned swine think Jesus was such a wonderful person? Why were those demons not just removed from the crazies, instead of causing a poor farmer to lose his entire herd of swine? The story doesn't seem fair to the owner of the swine and sounds like a fantasy.

Many similar questions have never been answered during the years that eleven-year old boy was growing up. Unanswered questions keep coming up and the list has become quite long. Preachers and others have tried, but their answers seem superficial and are not satisfactory. It is like living the life of a

---

[1] Matthew 8: 28-32

pilgrim, but making very slow progress. Struggling to find Truth is a lonesome and slow process. Struggling to find Truth in a Christian church is an exercise in frustration and conflicting stories when denied the right to ask difficult questions. Perhaps God intended the genuine pursuit of Truth for each thinking individual to be a difficult process. The church prefers a herd-mentality in the members: people that will not question the dogma developed by subjective human beings and presented as the authoritative belief of the Christian church, as received directly from God. If God did give us freedom of thought then why must our brains be shut down when entering a church? If people can truly find God through their own personal efforts perhaps the church authorities worry about their position and the hierarchy they have created. It is a hierarchy so far from the historical truth that it has created the 'Vacant Pew Syndrome' in Christian churches.

My true feelings were awful that night in the Methodist Church. What was wrong with me? What did the other kids experience that eluded me? The preacher was rated next to God in our town and I had let him down miserably. My parents never commented, but I could sense they were less than pleased with the evening. That eleven-year-old boy went home totally confused. He felt like a complete failure. His grades were good in school. Why couldn't he understand or comprehend what they said was such a simple truth and the greatest story ever told? Later in the week, I asked my father what he thought was wrong with me. He gave me a lecture I never forgot about being, "One of those unusual people that will not accept anything but proven facts. You believe nothing unless you can personally prove it to be true. Someday you may learn there are things that cannot be proven on that drafting table in your room or with mathematics." His words were burned into my brain. Why did my father think that his son was different? They were not comforting words for a new church member to hear coming from his father, the Sunday School Superintendent of the Knox Methodist Church.

That was the last time in my entire life there was ever a conversation about Christianity with my parents or the preacher. My dad and I enjoyed hunting and woodworking together. Christianity was always an off-limits subject we never discussed. There was something elusive about what they were teaching that did not make a connection within my brain cells. My brain must have been out there in the parking lot instead of inside my head while kneeling at the altar.

Over sixty-five years later, I am learning what the experience was supposed to be that night at the altar. What do people experience when they say they have been saved, or have Jesus Christ within them? Is it imagination, fantasy, mind control, or some other paranormal experience? It must be something beyond the laws of physics and biology that I was taught in college and cannot comprehend. Why is it beyond my capability? Subjects associated with accounting, engineering, and business are fairly complex and my grades were above average. Why can't I grasp and accept the overall concept the church teaches: *you must have faith and not ask questions.* Are they trying to conceal something? There are people that profess their Christianity regularly but couldn't pass a mathematics or biology test.

What is my problem? That is the question always on my mind and especially when in church. So far there have been no acceptable answers. Others have not been able to explain it in a manner that I can comprehend.

Preachers and theologians lament that Christian church participation is not growing. Some call it the 'Vacant Pew Syndrome.' Might the problem be similar to what I think the preacher may have inferred to that boy kneeling at the altar in 1933? "Leave your brain in the parking lot."

Christianity is not suggesting you leave your brain outside the church. In later life, I have concluded that is where the church wants your brain to be. When you ask too many questions some preachers will quickly remind you that this is a faith-based religion. You must accept the teaching of all miracles based on faith alone and please do not ask too many questions. When an ordained minister tells a person they must have faith alone they are not suggesting that you leave your brain in the parking lot. They are actually telling you it is precisely where your brain belongs. Thinking and questioning individuals are not the ones we welcome here. We want the non-thinkers and non-questioners that accept what we say as the gospel truth. The church has suppressed knowledge and scholarly works ever since the Roman Emperor Constantine chaired the meeting at Nicaea in 325 C.E. to develop the Nicene Creed (Apostle's Creed) for his personal advantage. He was not a Christian as the church teaches!

Scholars have known for centuries that the four gospels do not agree and differ widely on the subject material. They know the gospels have been drastically altered. Bishops, scribes, and others altered the *ancient mystery* teachings and presented it as the true Word of God as taught by Jesus and the disciples. A religion was created that is rigid and excludes every other human being unless they confess to Christianity as the only true religion, Jesus as their savior, born of a virgin, crucified, and ascended into heaven.

That is precisely what the Roman Emperor Constantine wanted when he presided over the Council of Nicaea. As the most ruthless Roman Emperor on record, he needed a means whereby the people could be controlled. Christianity did just that. It was a quid pro quo, because it gave the bishops the stature they wanted and the right to suppress all other religions, knowledge, and science of any kind. Free and open thought was absolutely forbidden. If you did not leave your brain outside of the church it would soon end up within a severed head. It provided Constantine the opportunity to proceed with his plundering and ruthlessness while knowing the populace was under the control of the church. Soldiers were no longer needed to control the masses after the church fathers were given the right to enforce their Christian religion by any means they desired. The church fathers were more effective in controlling the populace than soldiers or any police force could have been. Only church bishops and scribes were literate at the time of the Nicene Convention, which gave them absolute control over the populace. It was true genius on the part of Constantine.

It is no wonder the church grew so fast. People were exterminated if they did not profess Christianity. The result of the newly invented religion at the Council of Nicaea, Christianity, plunged the world into the Dark Ages for several centuries. On 20 May 325 C.E.[1] the Council even voted 218 to 2 (not unanimous) that from this day forward Jesus Christ will be known as a god and not a mortal prophet. Male-only representatives at the Nicene Council made the decision! One cannot help but wonder; would God have voted with the 218 for Jesus becoming a god that day or voted with all the dissenters? After all, HE is the only source of truth on that subject. Why were women excluded? How would women have voted? Patriarchal Christianity had relegated women to a subservient position. Prior to Christianity women were equal and at times rated higher than males. Christian churches still cannot agree if women have a right to preach the Gospel. That is ridiculous! Is the male hierarchy in Christianity afraid of women? It appears they are scared to death that women will overtake their positions and control. Most women known to me have far more empathy and compassion than males.

Lessons Learned in The Teen Boys Class

One reward of becoming a church member in 1933 was that it made boys eligible to become members of the Sunday school class taught by Victor Botts. Rumors were rampant in town about the subjects taught by Victor in the Teen Boys class of the Methodist Church. The excitement of becoming a church member was driven by the knowledge that boys could now join Vic's class and learn about the mysteries of what the rumors around town indicated he taught. No secret society could be better protected than the Teen Boys class. The older boys absolutely refused to divulge what they were learning.

---

[1] *Holy Blood, Holy Grail,* by Baigent, Leigh, and Lincoln, Dell books 1982

Victor Botts accepted me as the only new member from the catechism class. Unless you were approved by Vic there was no way a boy could join his class. Boys not approved by Vic had to attend a coed class, which was demeaning to their teenage manhood.

Vic had an agreement with the Sunday School Superintendent, my father, that no boy could attend his class unless he personally approved. It was a strange arrangement, but teachers for boys were difficult to enlist so Vic got his way. That first Sunday in Vic's class was a real shocker. He introduced me by telling the older boys that Kenton had passed his scrutiny and was now eligible for full participation and could be privy to all the things that he was teaching them. WOW! I thought this really is the big deal I was looking forward to by becoming a church member. After asking Vic why Jack and Ron had not joined the class he said, "They believe everything the preacher says and might not keep our subject material confidential."

The class met in a private room at the church with the door always closed. Vic told me to come forward and be properly initiated. He asked, "Do you honestly and sincerely desire to become a full-fledged member of the Teen Boys class?" "Yes sir, I do Mr. Botts," I said. "McElhattan don't call me that again," Vic said. He was in his late-twenties and it seemed polite to call him mister, but Vic did not approve. Then he said, "Put your hand on this Bible and repeat after me. Do you promise to never reveal any of the proceedings in this class or have discussions with anyone except other class members. Do you understand the entire class will take you down along Canoe Creek and beat the living hell out of you if you ever break any of the rules? If you agree and still want to be a full-fledged member of this class then say, I do."

Proceedings moved so fast and had taken me so much by surprise that I was afraid to say anything but, "I do." Vic told me I was now a full member of the Teen Boys class and to take a seat. During the next three years it became quite obvious there were many unwritten rules that were not explained that first day in the class. Peer pressure and a rough-tough-minded teacher can make a tremendous impression on teenage boys. We never heard of drugs in those days, but it is easy to understand what peer pressure can do to teenage boys and girls. As these words are being written there is still a guilt feeling that an oath of many years ago is being broken. What we learn as impressionable young people is difficult to remove from our memory. Perhaps it is even impossible. Since Victor and the other fellows are all now deceased maybe they will forgive me for writing about things we swore never to divulge. Getting the 'hell beat out of you' down along Canoe Creek by teenage peers can be demeaning and a bloody mess. I'm too old for that!

One boy that had talked too much later told his parents he fell off the railroad trestle that crosses Canoe Creek down by George "Beany" Whitehill's farm. Only Vic's Christian-teen-soldiers knew the truth.

Lessons learned in the Teen Boys class were the real stuff of life. Vic's teaching methods were crude by church or school standards but they sure left a lasting impression. His objective was to teach a bunch of normally unruly boys some simple facts of life that he had to learn the hard way. His father died during an influenza epidemic when Vic was a little boy. His mother washed clothes for people in her home to earn some money and couldn't give the kids much time. His older sister, Helen, was somewhat of a lady about town. Probably Vic got most of his knowledge about girls and sex from Helen. We never knew but it made fascinating material for Sunday lessons.

One memorable Sunday the lesson consisted of what a young gentleman never did with any girl unless you were married. Vic was still single but he seemed to know a lot about the opposite sex. We were instructed about the places you never touch a girl, along with Vic's personal threat that he would delight in "choking the crap out of us" if he ever learned we did such a thing to a girl. One of the older boys later reported that Vic's threat was a real obstacle when his girlfriend wanted to go the whole way one night while they were spooning in Peanut Park. He said that all he could think about were those big hands of Vic's around his neck choking him while his date was choking his manhood. The lesson was well learned, because she soon dumped him for another fellow. In the secret grading system, Vic put five gold stars after our classmate's name. Those big hands were far more impressive than 'Thou shall not covet.'

Another lesson was on the teachings of St. Paul; "do you not know that your body is a temple of the Holy Spirit within you, which you have from God?[1] You are not your own; you were bought with a price. So glorify God in your body." Also, "It is better to marry than to be aflame with passion."[2] "Don't ever forget men," Vic said, "and glorify God in the body of others and especially girls!" Vic called us men, because he always said that he was trying to beat some common sense into our thick turkey-like brains so we could mature into respectable men: "You are not little kids. When you are old enough to father children then you are a man." We didn't know much about fathering children, but sure had a genuine desire to learn. The gospel of St. Paul really didn't mean much to us with those turkey brains. The teacher was obviously aware of that. The gospel according to our 'Saint' Victor was,

---

[1] 1 Corinthians 6:19-20
[2] 1 Corinthians 7:9

"When you get aflame with sexual passion, then go and masturbate. Don't ever defile a girl by stealing her virginity for your personal pleasure. Just remember, I'm here to choke the crap out of you in case you forget." That we did understand, but were not too sure what virginity was all about. Of course, that led to another interesting lesson on a subject that may have been more appropriate for a biology class than Sunday school.

HURRY UP SON became a cliché in the class and later in town. Several weeks after becoming a member I got up enough nerve to speak up in class and report on what happened to me that night at the altar. Being the youngest guy in the class made me reluctant at first to speak-up. The older guys thought what happened to me was hilarious. Most of them had been to church that night the catechism class was accepted as new Methodist Christians. The joke was that they accused me of going to sleep at the altar. They teased me about not finding Jesus Christ that night, because I was sound asleep at the altar and Mrs. McCaskey had to waken me. "Boy! Did you hear McElhattan snore?" "No wonder the preacher wanted to get him out of there and back to his seat, he couldn't preach above that foghorn noise." "Hurry up son, wake up or you'll miss the train to heaven." Without realizing it my honesty started a trend in Hurry Up Son sayings, which were shortened to H'up Son. The joking wasn't devious or even about me. Instead, it put me in a position of envy by starting a new trend in our town.

My father's car was a 1929 model Hupmobile. Later when I learned to drive there were lots of fun jokes like, "that guy who slept at the altar is now trying to h'up to the preacher's heaven in a Hupmobile." The h'up term was used frequently. Only the initiated knew what it meant and where it came from and they were sworn to secrecy. In a complimentary manner statements were made like, "old McElhattan is the only guy that ever had enough guts to sleep at the altar while the preacher was trying to h'up and save his soul." "H'up son or some other clinker-head will date that girl."

Years later we still talked about Vic's Sunday school lesson on virginity. The lesson began with the question, "How many of you Turks[1] believe that God got Mary pregnant?" Not a hand went up. We didn't know what to do. Vic would pounce on you like a tiger if he disagreed with what you said. It was better to conceal your opinion than to be belittled before your peers. "If you think God got Mary pregnant without sex, raise your hand." Not a hand went up. "What's wrong with all you Turks, do you believe in the Bible?" All hands went up. "Boy! What a bunch of mixed-up clinker-head brains in this class. You don't know what you believe, do you?" A courageous older

---

[1] Short for turkey, a dumb barnyard bird.

fellow asked him if he believed Jonah had lived in the belly of a whale. "Absolutely not!" he answered, and, "I am pleased to learn you Turks are finally beginning to use that thing inside of your head called a brain. You must always question those Biblical fables that the preacher claims are facts, but cannot prove them to be true."

Victor Botts wasn't given much credit in town for having an over supply of brains. Even the Sunday School Superintendent knew that he spent most Saturday nights dancing and drinking at the Oil City Pulaski Club with the Polish girls. One night I overheard my dad ask mother what she thought about my Sunday school teacher. She told him, "Della Botts is a good hard-working woman and it would embarrass her to death if he asked Victor not to teach the class. Della is faithful in attending the Philathea class and is very proud to have a son teaching Sunday school." No action ever came from the conversation. It sure pleased me, because we were learning so much and could hardly wait for Sunday morning. No class could compete with the near perfect attendance of the Teen Boys, so why would the teacher be questioned? No one else wanted the job. How much my father knew I do not know. He did know that Vic was one of those 'diamonds in the rough' that attracted teenage boys to his class. Church school superintendents pray for that kind of teacher.

It had been rumored in town that some people's friends in Oil City had seen Victor Botts on various Saturday afternoons in the philosophy and religion section of the public library. That rumor was sure no surprise to those of us in the class. If he was getting all of this stuff we were being taught from the Oil City library then that made us proud that our teacher worked so hard preparing lessons. One Sunday a nosey woman said to him that she heard he was in the Oil City library. He told her that his girlfriend's mother thought her daughter was there and he went looking for her. It was a good answer but the wrong reason.

Victor Botts probably took his teaching of a boys Sunday school class more serious than anything he had ever done in his life. Kids don't respect many teachers. To have near perfect attendance and the close attention of unruly teenage boys must have given him a feeling of great personal pride. My opinion is that he took the job so serious that the library visits were to prepare him to pass along knowledge that was not available in either his home or the boys' home.

The biology we learned in the Teen Boys class was right on target with the teachings in college biology. Professor Bornhardt told our class at Ripon College that McElhattan was the only one to properly explain conception in the biology test. The professor liked to give preliminary tests before teaching a subject so he could learn how much the students already knew. He asked me to go to the blackboard and draw the diagram from my paper and explain the process. When finished he asked where I had gained that knowledge. I really could not bring myself to tell him that it was in a Methodist Church Sunday school class.

The explanation was that my father was raised on a farm about a mile out of town. Often I would walk out to granddad's farm. After watching my granddad and uncles help a cow give birth to a calf one day, they explained the entire process. Later my uncles, a few years older than me, made sure I knew the day when a cow was going to be bred. My grandmother seemed reluctant for me to go to the barn that day. If the cow being bred was a virgin she didn't seem to mind losing what they called virginity. It was sure obvious the bull enjoyed himself stealing her virginity. Of course, that was all reported in detail to the Teen Boys class, but not to the college biology class.

The truth was that Vic had gone into great detail on several Sundays, because he was convinced that Mary could not get pregnant by miraculous conception. The female ovum (egg) must be entered by one of several thousand male sperm to form a human embryo. When one sperm attaches then all others are rejected. The accepted sperm drops its tail and enters the ovum where the newly formed embryo starts the separation process, which begins the formation of a human being. Those Sunday school lessons were sensational for impressionable young boys. However, they did not agree with the Gospel teachings in the Bible.

Some fellows wanted to go with me to the farm. My uncles thought that was going too far. The questions planted into our 'thick turkey-brains' have never been answered satisfactorily. Perhaps they never will. Are we to believe the church teachings that on a one-time-only occasion God abrogated His divine biological facts and created a half-human and half-divine being? How could Jesus have a human genealogy that went back to David if the sperm came from God?

Mary couldn't get pregnant unless she supplied the ovum (egg) so was Jesus half-human from Mary's lineage and half-divine from the God-given sperm? Did God supply both the ovum and sperm for Mary? If so, why is God referred to as Father? Any dunce knows that fathers cannot produce an ovum. Hens lay eggs not roosters!

If God supplied both the egg and sperm then wouldn't that make Jesus both male and female? Perhaps God is a divine combination of all good things including both sexes and not patriarchal as the ancient Jews called Him. Women had no rights in ancient Judaism. They were male-owned property! Even today in a Judeo-Christian society we have inherited the custom of only the female being given away in a marriage ceremony.

Why isn't the male ever given away in a marriage ceremony? Is this a sexist thing that has carried over from ancient Judaism? Would male Christians lose control of the church if they abolished the custom? The tenth commandment certainly sounds like it is, *"You shall not covet your neighbors wife."*[1] Why is the tenth commandment silent on what a woman should do? Was God telling Moses that it is all right for a woman to covet her neighbor's husband?

Those were troubling subjects for teenage boys to discuss. Most of them were never answered satisfactorily as we developed into adults. Preachers will say that God meant all people should not covet not just men. The Ten Commandments and Gospels seem to have a definite male orientation, *"You have heard that it was said, 'You shall not commit adultery.' But I say to you that everyone that looks at a woman lustfully has already committed adultery with her in his heart."*[2] Is a woman permitted to look lustfully at a man and not commit adultery with him in her heart? In the ancient Egyptian mystical teachings women were always equal or superior to men. Those teachings predate Christianity by several thousand years and were accepted as mythical moral teachings that were acted out in allegorical pageantry.

Why do the Gospels go into human genealogical detail for Jesus if His genealogy is direct from God? Those were tough questions to ponder in the Teen-Boys class. They are still difficult today. We learned that the Gospels totally disagree on the genealogy of Jesus. In fact, they disagree on many items. Why would Pastor McCaskey say emphatically, **"This is the Word of God,"** before reading the Bible text for church? If it is the absolute Word of God then why couldn't He get it straight? Did God instruct different writers of the Bible Gospels to document things that do not agree? The preacher said to never question these things, "they are Biblical facts. If it is in the Bible then it is gospel truth." How can the words be gospel truth and completely disagree such as the genealogy of Jesus written in both Matthew[3] and Luke?[4]

Was the pastor telling us that God gave us freedom of speech and thought but when you enter his church that freedom is denied if you question anything about Christianity? We wanted to learn, not be rebuked. Teenagers have a real problem with documents that are supposed to be facts (gospel truth) when the documents do not agree.

It appears that the writer of St. Luke also had a problem. The preamble to

---

[1] Exodus 20:17
[2] Matthew 5:28
[3] Matthew 1:1-18
[4] Luke 3:23-38

the genealogy of Jesus states in verse 23 of the 3rd chapter, *"and Jesus himself began to be about thirty years of age, being (as was supposed) the son of Joseph, which was the son of Heli."* AS WAS SUPPOSED in parenthesis makes it appear that the writer was not very sure of his facts. According to Matthew he wasn't within a country mile of being correct or else Matthew is wrong.

Kids love this kind of a problem when adults tell them they are reading facts but the two fact sources do not agree. Preachers may not know it happens but kids sit there and chuckle to himself/herself thinking this holy guy in the pulpit really doesn't know anymore about it than I do. He wants me to accept everything he says and what is written in the Bible as literal truth and not question his material. However, his source book doesn't even agree between chapters. You better 'Hurry Up Son' and get that turkey-brain of yours out into the parking lot or you will leave this place totally confused. Perhaps lay people should not be permitted to read the Bible.

Vic was a maverick and loved to have his class get into heated debates about Biblical inconsistencies. If he contributed nothing else, Vic certainly left others and me with a lifelong suspicion about the accuracy of any written words in the Bible and religious documents. It was fun to debate the possibilities of what may happen if the dime-novel stories about Buck Rogers and Doc Savage were actually true. Paperback dime novels were all the rage in the days before television became a reality. Many of us did not have the ten cents to buy one. Some Sundays Vic would ask what we wanted the lesson to be about the following week. If the consensus were Buck Rogers then he would buy the ten-cent paperback book and give a full report. Wrist radios, space travel, rocket ships to the moon, and other fantasies were 'hot items' for teenagers to dream about in the nineteen thirties. We even thought a husband was required to have a baby!

How could we know that many of those fantasies would become realities due to the trouble brewing in Germany that resulted in World War II? Pre-war teenagers were living in a time period that created a generation gap between them and their children. A time before television, plastic, credit cards, frozen food, ballpoint pens, laser beams, micro-wave ovens, electric blankets, air conditioners, drip-dry clothes, fast food, clothes dryers, pantyhose, polio shots, penicillin, the pill, radar, FM radio, tape decks, electric typewriters, artificial hearts, computers, word processors, group therapy, day care centers, sex changes, and many more. Our progeny may think we were living in a time warp.

Florence L. Ditty   Kenton E. McElhattan
June 1945, Knox, Pennsylvania
Photo at McElhattan home

We hope our children, grandchildren, and great-grandchildren do not think that we were living in an 'age of innocence' or a time warp. Depression-age children did not have many material things, but we did have love and respect for one another including our parents, relatives, friends, and especially the schoolteachers.

World War II

B-24 Liberator Crew. Photograph taken February 1945, prior to leaving from Topeka, Kansas to fly the new M-model plane to England for combat missions in the 8th Air Force. First row left to right: D.E.Atkins, P.G.Berkley, K.E.McElhattan, N.Bohnick, S.A.Reisman, C. Richards. Standing left to right: F.Renekowitz, R. Rodda, C.G. Geiger, L.M. Tinsley

B-24 Liberator Bombers, 458th Bomb Group, 752nd Squadron (red-white-red tails) flying home to Horsham St. Faith, Norwich, England on April 25, 1945. This was last mission flown in WWII by the 8th Air Force. Target: Railroad marshalling yard at Bad Reichenhall, Austria. Bombs on target: 140.1 Tons. Airborne: 11.8 hours. K. E. McElhattan was in a 752nd Squadron B-24 Liberator. In 1964 he traveled with Karl Heinz-Stettner to evaluate German coalmines for mechanization. Karl was a German anti-aircraft gunner at Bad Reichenhall. Both men agreed they were blessed that Karl had missed our B-24, and that our bombs hit the target–not German gunners.

Following High School graduation it was possible for me to complete a twelve-month accounting course at Franklin Commercial College by painting, clerking in a grocery store, and some part time work at Knox Glass Bottle Company to earn money for tuition. It was a good course. Only years later when active in business management did I realize how important the accounting education would be. It is a pity that engineering school students are not even taught the difference between debits and credits. Knowledge of balance sheets, profit and loss statements, inventory, and cost control are vital business subjects for an engineer to understand before he can assume senior management responsibility.

On December 7, 1941, when Pearl Harbor was bombed, Knox Glass had me working as head of the accounting/billing group at the executive office in Oil City, PA. Getting a job in the executive office of the glass company was 'heady-stuff' in those days. Mr. Roy R. Underwood was the founder-president of the company. He was faithful about attending our Methodist Church on Sunday. After church he always went to his office at Knox for about an hour. My Sunday pattern was to rush out of church and beat him to the office and be waiting on the front steps when he arrived. My question was the same every Sunday after a pleasant hello, "Mr. Underwood, have you found an opening for me yet where I can use my accounting schooling?" Some people that knew about my Sunday procedure thought it took a lot of guts and probably someday RR, as he was known, would kill me. We had learned in Victor Botts Teen Boys Class that if you really want something bad enough that is a worthy cause then don't let 'hell or high water' stand in your way. RR had built the company from nothing and never left 'hell or high water' stand in his way. A company founder understands determination!

After several Sundays of harassment, as some called it, Mr. Underwood invited me into his office. His words are still clear in my mind, "McElhattan you have been a genuine pain in the ass for the past several weeks. To get rid of you every Sunday, you are to report to Ed Schrag, Executive Vice President, in the Oil City office at nine o'clock tomorrow morning. Now get the hell out of here and let me do some work, and don't be waiting for me next Sunday on the office steps." Mr. Underwood was asked if Mr. Schrag had a job for me. "Son, if you irritate him the way you have me you will probably be asked to go jump in the Allegheny River. That bridge in Oil City is high enough to either break your damn neck or drown," he said.

The next morning in Oil City, Ed Schrag told me I was to start immediate training to replace the head of the billing department who was being transferred to one of the glass factories as chief accountant. Also, he told me, "As you know, RR doesn't have any children. It is confidential, but a nephew of his had to be fired from the training due to plain laziness. He thought he was a big shot just because his uncle was the company president. It was quite an embarrassment for the president to be wrong. Although you are young, RR thinks you may have enough guts to fight with railroads on boxcar freight rates and keep salesmen from cheating on their expense reports." Mr. Schrag also told me, "if you fail in this position I would be pleased to personally throw you off the Oil City Bridge into the Allegheny River." Apparently Schrag and RR had discussed the matter in some detail.

What Mr. Schrag didn't know was that my Sunday determination was partly due to knowing all about RR's nephew problem. Small towns have few secrets. Even RR's wife had told some women in my mother's Sunday school ladies Philathea Class about the problems with her nephew. Not many local people were ever accepted in the Knox Glass Executive Office, which made it a genuine challenge for me to succeed locally in a small town. Vic Botts and others that were previously in the Teen Boys class knew what was going on.

Chronological Notes From WWII Events
(From notes written during WWII)

August 2, 1942, Sunday. 20th birthday. Now eligible to enlist in Air Force without parental consent.

August 3, 1942, Monday. Skipped lunch with people from Knox Glass and went to recruiting office to enlist in the Air Force. Personal research indicates the Army Air Force is best opportunity for schooling in the armed forces. Told Mr. Schrag I would be leaving in two to three weeks when called-up.

August 7, 1942, Friday. Mr. Underwood returned from a trip. He and Schrag talked with me about the company applying for a deferment. I assured them John Kribbs was very capable and qualified to manage the billing department, which they accepted.

August 22, 1942, Saturday. Ordered to active duty and reported to Oil City Recruiting Office. To Erie, PA by bus for physicals at armory. Late afternoon by troop train to Fort Meade, Maryland. One week at Meade taking mental tests, physicals, and shots then by troop train to St. Petersburg, Florida.

Late August to mid-October 1942. Clearwater, Florida in Bel-Aire Hotel (world's largest wooden hotel) doing basic training every day on golf course.

Mid-October 1942. Shipped by troop train to Chanute Field, Rantoul, Illinois. Next three months attending Air Force Technical School. My classes are 11:00 pm to 7:00 am. Hoot Owl shift. Most instructors are Civil Service civilians. Four in our class asked to attend Instructors Training School. Several G.I. teachers are needed, because civilians have no authority over Air Force personnel except in class.

January 30, 1943.   Presented Certificate of Qualification for Air Force Technical School Instructor under civilian Civil Service program.

February 1, 1943.   After one week furlough started teaching subjects of drafting, geometry, cadmium plating, aircraft maintenance and repair, sheet-metal and plexi-glass layout and forming, self-sealing fuel tanks, aircraft cable splicing, and machine shop techniques. Instructors are permanent party so I applied and was accepted as bass horn player in Air Force Band. Saw my first B-24 Bomber land and pull up to our hangar for a sheet-metal wing repair. Working on the "Old Girl" I fell madly in love with her. Talking with the crew about their life and flying experiences created fantasies about how could I ever qualify to be one of the flight crew on such a beautiful aircraft. It seems impossible.

May 1943.   Took four days of intensive tests in attempt to qualify for ASTP (Army Specialized Training Program). Fear that our country would have a generation of non-college educated men due to the war.   After qualifying, my commanding officer told me that I am 'plain nuts.' He had submitted my name for OCS (Officers Candidate School) and wanted to personally sponsor me. I explained how much his confidence in me was appreciated, but OCS would disqualify me for any college program while in the armed service. He got more than a little upset when I reminded him that OCS required a minimum IQ of 110 and ASTP required an IQ of 120 or higher. It was just plain facts, not an attempt to put officers down.

Scholars in Foxholes

Scholars in Foxholes by Louis E. Keefer, 1988 COTU Publishing, Reston, Virginia is the story of the Army Specialized Training Program in World War II. Commonly known as ASTP. It provided many young men a college education they never would have received otherwise. It was an opportunity to fulfill my obsession for a Mechanical Engineering education.

Excerpts from *Scholars in Foxholes*

Page 18: The Army had to demand of its trainees in ASTP the fullest possible concentration of time and energy in highly accelerated and no-frills courses. No extra curricular activities are permitted.

Page 19: Quoting General George C. Marshall, "The Army has been increasingly handicapped by a shortage of men possessing desirable combinations of intelligence, aptitude, education, and training in the fields such as medicine, engineering, languages, science, mathematics, and psychology, who are qualified for service as officers of the Army. The Army was compelled to assure itself that there would be no interruption in the flow of professionally trained and technically trained men who have hitherto been provided in regular increments by American colleges and universities."

Page 45: Quoting various college presidents, "we especially liked the young ASTP scholars themselves. They are alert, bright, capable and attentive. The most earnest groups of young men that it has ever been my pleasure to be associated with. They work much harder than our civilian students and like it."

Page 76: "Besides being highly accelerated—more than double the normal college pace—many ASTP curricula involved such demanding subjects as physics, chemistry, and various courses in advanced mathematics. Classroom work required concentrated study, and especially in the engineering curriculum, the completion of long homework assignments involving extensive reading and problem solving. Moreover, engineering trainees mostly made their necessary computations manually because 'log-log duplex decitrig' slide rules were not always available, and today's hand held calculators were yet to be invented."

Page 125: Quoting General Walter L. Weible, "ASTPers had higher average test scores than either Air Cadets or candidates at West Point and the Naval Academy, and they also have to work harder."

Late May and June 1943. Sent to ASTP at the University of Illinois, Champaign-Urbana, Illinois for intensive courses in mathematics and chemistry. When completed sent to Ripon College at Ripon, Wisconsin for total immersion in Basic Engineering then Advanced Engineering curriculum. Total of 200 men in ASTP program at Ripon College. All in the same class, but different courses. No civilians in any classes except one girl in a biology class. She was brilliant and could keep up with the intellectual pace, but a bit flaky otherwise. Not dating material! ASTP college credits earned in less than one-half normal college time. Life consists of class and laboratory work, studying, taking tests, eating, and very little sleep. Professors will often give tests on several chapters ahead of where we are in classroom work. If you complain the standard answer is, "If you are not smart enough to stay several chapters ahead of where I teach in class then you should not be here." Recreation consists of horsing around in the dormitory and whistling at girls as we march past their dorms on the way to class.

April 1, 1944. Completed Advanced Engineering at Ripon and given diploma by W. H. Barber, Registrar and Major Thomas R. Barner, Commandant along with 194 other fellows that made it. Five men failed.

Prior to graduation everyone in the class was given a full week of intensive tests to determine if we could qualify for medical school. Two of us qualified and sent immediately to the University of Michigan at Ann Arbor for medical school. Soon learned the regimen at Ripon College was easy compared to the medical curriculum at Michigan. The twenty-five in our class are so totally immersed in quantitative and qualitative chemistry, biology, anatomy, zoology, and laboratory work that our dean discourages any contact, whatsoever, with anyone except our peers or upper classmen. We almost forgot that girls even existed.

July 1944.   Completed first semester of medical school. Decided I should get into active combat rather than become a professional student. Our First Sergeant became a confidential friend. He told me about an unpublished regulation whereby anyone applying for active combat in an Air Force bomber crew would take priority over any other assignment. WOW! My opportunity to fulfill the many months of fantasy about active duty on a B-24 Liberator bomber. The dean tried to stop me from leaving medical school. The First Sergeant was correct about the unpublished regulation and the dean had no choice but to acquiesce to the Army Regulation.

August 1944.   Sent to Wichita Falls, Texas for orientation about flight status and a battery of tests. Later in month sent to Tyndall Field, Florida to begin aerial gunner training. Training is intensive. Flying everyday is what some of us call being in "hog heaven." Training on B-17 Bombers, which I learned to dislike very much. A nutty pilot missed getting one wheel on the concrete and we had a 'pancake landing.' Spent several days in the infirmary with a bruised shoulder and nearly lost flying status. The pilot had flown 50 combat missions over Germany and was 'flak-happy' and careless.

October 20, 1944.   Presented Flight Crew Wings and given a 10 day furlough. My parents were shocked when I showed up at home sporting a nice shiny pair of wings. Didn't want to worry them so they were not told about the training to be a flight crewmember. Initially assigned to nose turret. Schooling qualified me for Aerial Flight Engineer, but need more flying hours. Any assignment was appreciated to become a B-24 Liberator flight crewmember. One night in Knox I was matching pennies at the local coffee shop hangout with two girls from my high school class. That was about all of the excitement you could find in a small town during the war. Florence Ditty and Mary Jane Weible cleaned me out of money. Thankfully some money had been left at home or they would have made me a poverty case for the Air Force to deal with. If it takes the rest of my life, I promised myself to get even with them. After walking home with them it was obvious I had been rather stupid not to pay more attention to Florence Ditty while in school.

During that furlough we went to several movies together, which confirmed my stupidity in high school. As the time came for the furlough to end I dreaded leaving town and the nice girl from our high school class. The truth is she was popular and avoided me in high school, because I worked all the time and didn't attend social activities.

November 1944.   Reported to Lincoln, Nebraska for assignment to an aircrew then sent to Boise, Idaho for 90 days flight training to become an efficient B-24 Bomber (Liberator) flight crewmember. We were in the air every day with the exception of Thanksgiving when all planes were grounded due to a snowstorm. Flying so many hours in the Pacific NW is a wonderful experience. Our nine crewmembers are like a family. We're trained to react that the aircraft and other men's lives are more important to save than our own life in an emergency. That mental attitude is precisely how I got my fingers frozen. At high altitude over the Rocky Mountains one-night two power packs for the engines turbo super charger failed. With only two engines out of the four running my flying gloves were ripped off to quickly install the power packs to start the engines. Thermometer was showing a minus 54° F.

February 1945.   In mid-month our crew was transferred to Topeka, Kansas for assignment to a new B-24 Liberator, M model, to fly and break-in while awaiting orders for overseas. We put a total of six hours on our new plane before starting to Europe.

March 4, 1945.   Flying the North Atlantic Ocean in winter is a dangerous undertaking. We're young and have supreme confidence in our ability and the B-24 Liberator, so it never enters our minds to worry. Every aircrew member carries a Colt Automatic .45 caliber handgun in a shoulder holster. We were not issued ammunition until entering our bomber prior to leaving Bangor.   The reason given was that previous crews had been issued ammunition while still in the barracks and used the light bulbs for target practice. We were sorry to learn that our crew had missed that fun.

Before leaving, each soldier could purchase a carton of candy, cigarettes, and chewing gum, which were rationed in the United States. We give most of the candy and chewing gum to children that hang around our airfield at Norwich England. (Horsham St. Faith Airfield)   It's a thrill to see the smiles and how happy a stick of gum or a candy bar makes the kids.

In 1994 an article was written for the *Second Air Division History Book* about a B-24 Liberator engine on our flight to Wales. The POE (Port Of Embarkation) was Bangor, Maine. The following article covers the period of time from March 4, 1945 to March 20, 1945, which was the sixteen days it took us to fly to Wales.

Maine to Wales in Sixteen Days!
(Written for Second Air Division History Book, 1994)
By Kenton E. McElhattan (13088635)

Near Three Rivers Stadium, in Pittsburgh, Pennsylvania a large neon sign spells out the letters **C • L • A • R • K.** The Clark Candy sign is a daily reminder that B-24 Bombers were forced out of the sky during WWII by more mundane things than enemy bullets or anti-aircraft fire.

Heavy Bombardment Crew Number FA-155AA-6, B-24 Project Number 9303OR, Airplane Serial Number 44-50798, was ordered to destination APO 19144AA. In layman's language we were to fly our newly acquired B-24 M from Topeka, Kansas to Bangor, Maine then on to Anglesey, Wales via Goose Bay, Labrador and Reykjavik, Iceland. It seemed like a rather simple no-brain assignment for a crew with 90 days flight training at Boise, Idaho then at Topeka, Kansas where we flew our new B-24 Liberator the sum-total of six-hours.

On March 4, 1945, the great excitement on the leg to Bangor was using the Relief-Tube over Cleveland, Ohio. It was our method of showing humble respect to a crewmember that talked too frequently about the attributes of his home city. Paul Berkeley never forgave us; however, we were all relieved after a ritual of the "Tube Over Cleveland." Upon arrival at Bangor, the aircraft log of problems was quite long. Youth and supreme confidence in our B-24 Liberator made us rationalize problems that could be disastrous by commercial airline standards.

Over Northern New Brunswick on March 6 at 0937 hours the #2 engine started pumping oil from the filler cap on top of the wing. The aileron, rudder, and elevator were working just fine and did not need the extra lubricant from the engine. Number 2 engine was feathered. Emergency radio instructions ordered a 180-degree turn; proceed to Presque Isle, Maine; attempt landing. We made it into the small civilian airport on three engines with no problems. Ground staff reported a B-17 had landed there about 18 months ago after three attempts. That statement reinforced our already exaggerated confidence in the performance of B-24 Liberators. We found nothing wrong with #2 engine and were back in the air in less than one hour. Timing was critical due to limited daylight in which to land a bomber at Goose Bay, Labrador.

Airborne and over New Brunswick again the #2 engine started ejecting oil from the filler cap. Upon landing the second time at Presque Isle it seemed like the whole town was out to greet us with fire trucks and all. In the dark and bitter cold that night we found the culprit! Someone at Willow Run, Ford Motor Plant left the wrapper from a Clark Bar candy bar in the oil tank. The candy wrapper must have shifted positions in the oil tank and acted like a valve, which created enough pressure to force oil out the filler cap. We spent the night in a small hotel at Presque Isle.

The townspeople were most friendly and kind to provide food for a big meal. They overwhelmed our crew with generosity. During a late night discussion we learned how proud they were for Presque Isle to be the Northern-most airfield in the USA. Also, townspeople insisted that Aroostook County produced bigger and better potatoes than where we had trained in Idaho. Headed for combat, we hated to leave our new friends the next day.

We finally found Goose Bay by our tail-gunner reporting a red streak in the snow after being hopelessly lost and without any radio contact. The radio compass kept indicating we were close to an airfield on each turning maneuver; all we could see was snow. The geniuses on the ground forgot to brief us at Bangor that water with red dye had been poured down the center of the runway, on top of the packed snow, for identification. Thanks to Chuck Richard being alert in the tail turret we made the airstrip instead of ending up in a snowdrift.

Goose Bay weather was sunny, no clouds, and about 15° F in mid-day. Some of us went ice fishing each day. We caught enough smelt that the Mess-Sergeant prepared them special for our crew. He took great pride in preparing the fresh fish dinner each evening and ate with us as part of the agreement. Also, he "slipped" us bacon for bait! Fumes in the Nissan-hut oil furnaces were so bad that four of us slept in our B-24 each night. Our extra load was GI[1] blankets and K-Rations, so there was plenty to eat and blankets to keep warm. Unfortunately, the North Sea storms and bad weather at Reykjavik cleared after nine days so we had to leave that winter paradise. We were told that a sergeant who was overlooked in the two-year rotation plan out of Goose Bay refused to get on the C-43 taking him back to the States. He insisted that the wheels were too small to run all the way back to the USA. Sedatives relaxed him from the snow-madness and helped him sleep on the flight home.

---

[1] GI means Government Issue

On March 16 we finally landed in Iceland. It was a boring place with stark terrain that time of year. Many Icelanders were pro-German so transient crews were restricted to the airbase. For four days the dice and cards were given the old GI workout due to a severe North Atlantic storm that kept all planes grounded. Headed for combat, we concluded why be in a hurry?

It was a glorious day on March 20, 1945, at our POA (Port Of Arrival) Anglesey, Wales. After the foul weather in Iceland and snow in Labrador it seemed like a paradise. Coming in low over the Isle of Man the lush green terrain was a welcome sight. We were greeted by the ground crew telling us that 16 days to fly from Maine to Wales must be some kind of a record. Completing the trip and overcoming problems was an achievement. The North Atlantic crossing provided an ideal means to shakedown new aircraft headed for European combat.

'Rosy the Riveter' and thousands of other dedicated Americans turned out B-24 Liberators at the rate of one every 90 minutes. The B-24 Liberator was the most highly produced military aircraft in American history. There were 19,256 B-24 Bombers of various models manufactured. Flight crews rarely complained about production problems. We knew that our fellow-countrymen were sacrificing and working long hours to produce those wonderful "Old Girls" that some of us were privileged to fly. A neon sign in Pittsburgh flashing the name CLARK is a pleasant reminder of one interesting in-flight problem a B-24 Liberator crew experienced on their trip to European combat with the 8th Air Force. It is a reminder of a period in time during American history when everyone worked together for the demise of the Third Reich, and the preservation of DEMOCRACY.

End of article.

March 21, 1945. After a nights sleep we went by train to Norwich, England, Horsham St. Faith Air Base home of the 458th Bombardment Group of the Eighth Air Force. Our crew was assigned to the 752nd Squadron consisting of twelve B-24 Liberator Bombers. There are four squadrons in a Bomb Group so we had 48 planes in our group at Horsham St. Faith.

March 22 to April 10, 1945. Training and orientation for combat flying included practice bomb runs over the English Channel, ditching training, map reading, ground escape procedures, etc. Without a bombardier, the Nose

Turret gunner was given full responsibility for the bomb load and for dropping the bombs, because US Air Force had gone to pattern bombing. On the bomb-run to target I followed procedure of the Bombardier in the lead Aircraft. Required extra training. Following are missions flown.

[1]**April 11, 1945.**   TARGET: Regensburg, Germany. Total bomb tons dropped on mission was 180.5 tons by 79 aircraft, 5 aircraft damaged, no aircraft losses, 22 KIA (killed in action), P-51 Mustang fighter coverage.

April 14, 1945.   TARGET: Pointe deGrave, France.   336 Aircraft dispatched to target with 1,000 pound "blockbusters." Total tonnage 1,246 tons. Planes stripped of all machine guns, armament, and only a 5-man crew to reduce weight for heavy bomb load.   Allied ground troops over-ran Germans holed up in concrete pillboxes.   Objective to produce cracks in pillboxes and hit the same target with Napalm (jelly fire bombs) tomorrow. No aircraft loss, no KIA.   Extra training required for me tonight for orientation on Napalm Bombs and how to arm them at high altitude.

April 15, 1945.   TARGET: Pointe deGrave & Rowan, France.   359 Aircraft dispatched carrying Napalm in P-51 belly tanks. 18 Aircraft aborted and dumped their load in the English Channel, because Napalm expanded at altitude and P-51 tanks had been filled to the top. I cracked-open the bomb bay doors for ventilation and scraped napalm into oxygen boxes to throw out over target. Bombs were armed at 25 feet from plane on descent. Thankful I had to take extra training to handle napalm bombs. No Aircraft losses, No KIA. First and only use of napalm in Europe. Battle Star for this mission.

April 16, 1945.   TARGET: Airfield at Landshut, Germany.   273 Aircraft dropped 679.8 tons of bombs.   Very heavy anti-aircraft fire.   One plane lost. No KIA reported on returning aircraft. Received the official Air Force photo after VE Day that confirms bombs were dropped at 18,800 feet and made direct hit at 11:49 A.M. Germans low on fuel so no enemy aircraft dispatched.

April 18, 1945.   TARGET: Passau, Germany, major railroad center. 166 Aircraft dropped 372.3 tons of bombs. Extremely heavy anti-aircraft fire. No losses in our bomb group.

April 20, 1945. TARGET: Zweisel, Germany, railroad center.   56 Aircraft dropped 123.5 tons of bombs. Extremely heavy anti-aircraft fire but no losses of any type.

April 25, 1945. LAST HEAVY BOMBER MISSION IN EUROPE. TARGET: Bad Reichenhall, Austria. 56 Aircraft dropped 140.1 tons of

---

[1] As officially written in the Army Air Force records for Targets, Aircraft, bomb tonnage and losses.

bombs to knock out a railroad center in the mountains where German troops were being evacuated. Very heavy anti-aircraft fire due to concentration of German guns. Damage to our plane, flak in nose turret. There were 19 other B-24's heavily damaged but no loss of life. Longest mission flown by 8th Air Force out of England. We were airborne 11.8 hours. 48 planes on the airbase taking off at 30 second intervals meant the first plane had 24 minutes less fuel by the time number 48 was in the air. After landing we ran out of fuel before getting to the parking area. Most of the 458th Group planes landed in France to refuel in order to get home. Flight plan took us 6 miles northwest of Munich (Munchen), directly over Chiemsee Lake (shaped like the head of a Scotty Dog). After bomb-run, diversion took us over Berchtesgaden, (Hitler's mountain hideout) circled over north Italy, then direct to Horsham St. Faith. The day started at 2:30 A.M.

May 7, 1945.   VE Day (Victory in Europe, Germans surrendered).

April 26 to June 11, 1945.   Volunteered and flew 'Trolley Missions' over France and Germany. Low-level flights to let ground personnel and P51 Mustang pilots view bomb damage.   Started training for Pacific warfare. Volunteered to fly in aircraft where co-pilots were being checked out as pilots. Took all in-flight tests to get official rating for Aerial Flight Engineer (748) and received that rating.

June 12, 1945.   Started first leg of trip to USA with our crew of 9 plus 10 ground personnel as passengers. We were being rushed back to receive B-29 training before going to the Pacific theater of warfare. Landed at Stornoway, Scotland, in the Hebrides Islands and spent two nights there due to horrible weather. Left for Iceland the second day. Weather got very bad and we could not get above or below the storm; bad icing conditions; 10 ground personnel were not equipped for high altitude flying; nothing to navigate by; Greg Geiger, the pilot, later confirmed we had been over 500 miles off-course and located Iceland by pure luck. Sun was shining 24 hours a day in Iceland. We got a few hours sleep and left for Goose Bay, Labrador.

June 19, 1945.   Landed at Westover Field, Springfield, MA. We saw our first helicopter while taxiing-in at Westover. A Texas ground man had been so cold in our bomber the past seven days that he kissed the ground and swore he would never get into another airplane as long as he lived. Given furlough and ordered to report to Sioux Falls, South Dakota on July 22. Florence Ditty was the main attraction for me in Knox during that furlough.

August 15, 1945.   Japan surrendered. Started on troop train next day for Harlingen, Texas for B-29 training. Did not get training at Harlingen due to war being over. Stayed there with nothing to do until being sent to Newark,

New Jersey and discharged on November 2, 1945. My great disappointment of WWII was not getting the training and flying time required for Crew Chief (Flight Engineer) on a B-29 Bomber. It would have fulfilled what my commanding officer at Chanute Field wanted for me. The Flight Engineer on a B-29 was an officer. We were enlisted men on a B-24.

Discharge reads:

>Battles and Campaigns: Rhineland, Central Europe, Air Combat (Royan Raid-Napalm)
>Decorations/Citations: European-African-Middle Eastern Ribbon w/3 Bronze Stars, Good Conduct and Air Medal
>Qualification Record: Aerial Flight Engineer (748), Gunner (611)
>Rank: Sergeant
>Aviation Badge (Technical School Instructor)
>Flight Crew Wings and Aerial Gunner Wings
>Pistol Qualification: 45 caliber (for aircraft)
>Separation Base: Newark, NJ
>Mustering out pay: Total of $163.21

What Greatest Generation?

The generation of men and women living during WWII has been referred to as the greatest generation.[1] Most people from that generation simply do not believe they were a great generation. It was a generation in transition between a less complex time period and one when many things were changed due to technological advances. The next generation must always be the greatest generation. If each new generation is not superior to the previous one then mankind will regress. Each generation must re-fight the battles and bring new vitality to the ideals that their parents and grandparents cherish, or allow those ideals to decay. The task for young people is to continuously recreate the ancient values through their own individual efforts and behavior.[2]

Knowing how to use the future requires an understanding of the past. We should learn from the mistakes of our ancestors. God repeatedly lamented, as revealed through the prophets, that His people had such short memories, and did not learn from their father's mistakes. Biblical people viewed ancestry as very important, because they would learn where they came from, learn the ancient values to which each new generation must bring new

---

[1] Brockaw, Tom, *The Greatest Generation*
[2] McElhattan, K.E., *Our Line©1987*

vitality, and learn that in the end each person belongs only to the family of God.

Young people learn habits, attitudes, and ways of judging through intense personal relationships with family, peers, or role models. They do not learn ethical principles on their own. They do emulate either ethical or unethical people. Young people, both in their environment and in their imaginative life require role models. They relate to people that have good characteristics and are models of people at their best. [1]

A generation can only be a great generation if it provides ethical family, peers, or role models for young people. Mankind will regress if only unethical family, peers, or role models are available in any generation. People that became adults during the early years of WWII only did what any generation has done before them in the recorded history of mankind. They were people performing at their best, making the most of their inherited characteristics, and the tools available to them during the era in which they lived.

Like so many great historical events, the generation of WWII had a common cause. They believed in Democracy. They were people willing to sacrifice their lives for Freedom in America. People living during the WWII era cannot be called a greater generation than any other just because they believed that America should continue to be a free country. Didn't the men and women that made major sacrifices during the American Revolution believe in the same cause? Soldiers lost their lives during the Civil War for believing in the cause that black people should also be free and not slaves in the United States of America.

My great-grandfather, Eli Berlin, was killed on July 2, 1863, in the Battle of Gettysburg, because he believed that President Abraham Lincoln was correct. Eli served in Company G of the Eighty-Third Regiment, Pennsylvania Volunteers from Tionesta, PA. The flag he was carrying when shot is on display in the Tionesta Historical Society Museum. His young widow was left with five little boys and one girl on a remote farm in Forest County, Pennsylvania. The boys were later sent to Soldier's Orphan Schools.

The Greatest Generation may be a good title for selling books. It is a patently unfair statement about our American ancestors. It is comforting to know that people of that generation do not believe it was a great generation, and are embarrassed by the use of that reference to them.

---

[1] Ibid.

Post World War II

Following WWII and marriage to the wonderful girl, Florence Ditty, who made furloughs more meaningful, we moved to Rocky Grove a suburb of Franklin, PA. The man across the street came over while moving into the house at Rocky Grove. He appeared a few years older than me. "I'm Cy Moorhead, welcome to the community," he said. "I work at the Rocky Grove Presbyterian Church. If there is anything I can do now or later just let me know." After thanking him and saying I am a Methodist beyond hope, I went into the house and told Florence that the Presbyterian Church janitor lived across the street. To my chagrin, I learned a few days later that Cy was the pastor of the church not the janitor.

During the next few months Pastor Cyrus Moorhead became a good friend but we did not attend his church. We were not active in a church at that time. We belonged to the Knox Methodist Church, which was twenty-two miles away. Many evenings Cy would come over and help me saw boards or watch me operate the wood lathe that had been set-up in the attic.

Cy was excited to see what could be turned on a lathe. He didn't know anything about wood lathes so I taught him how to operate it. Some days we would sit in the attic talking until two or three in the morning. Our wives were not too pleased and probably thought we were a couple of idiots. Invariably, our discussions would go from woodworking to religion. He was interested in my WWII Army Air Force activities, but I never told him much about it. He was more than a little surprised to learn that I had never met an army chaplain during my service career. I told him the Air Force probably didn't want us to get too friendly with those angels while flying high altitude up there in angel territory. Flak from anti-aircraft guns and bullets from German fighter planes didn't seem like angel territory to bomber crews. Our angels were the nurses and British girls in the pubs after bombing missions.

Pastor Moorhead was such a common man that he did seem more like a janitor than a stuffed shirt Presbyterian preacher. My grandmother Berlin did not like Presbyterian preachers. As her only male heir and next-door neighbor she had a great influence on me. She was an unforgiving Methodist that thought all Presbyterians were conceited and taught predestination.

She knew a preacher (Presbyterian) that had taken a drink of liquor one time and could not understand how he had the nerve to ever stand at the pulpit again. She thought the world was going straight to Hell's fire and brimstone eternity after Prohibition was repealed. I'm sure that my early life aversion to Presbyterians was due to her influence.

After telling Cy about mistaking him for the janitor he said that in many ways the janitor actually did more visible good in the church than the preacher. Cy thought it was hilarious after I learned to trust him enough to talk a little bit about the Knox Methodist Church Teen Boys class. Sex education in a boy's Sunday school class was a first to his knowledge. I couldn't divulge the teacher's name because he was still alive. It was a surprise to learn that Cy was not at all critical. In his calm and unassuming manner he said that God works in mysterious ways and perhaps someday the boys from that class would benefit from such an unconventional teacher.

About a year after moving, I got up enough nerve to suggest we attend the Rocky Grove Presbyterian Church next Sunday. It was not a comfortable thought to enter a Presbyterian Church. After our son Kent was born, Florence and I agreed it was our obligation as parents to raise children in a Christian home, or at least a home where the parents attended church. Also, curiosity about my new woodworking friend and the late night Bible discussions overcame my reluctance to visit a Presbyterian Church. Later, Cy told me that he was shocked to see me in his church with my wife and infant son that first Sunday morning. So was I!

The service didn't seem much different than in our Methodist Church. After some announcements, Pastor Moorhead entered the pulpit and said before reading the Bible text; *"This is the word of God, as written by man."* That was different! Pastor McCaskey had never added **'as written by man'** and neither did his successor Pastor Thompson who married us, but I never got to know him very well.

Why did Cy add those words? While hearing my first sermon in a Presbyterian Church my thoughts were primarily centered on the words **"as written by man"** instead of the sermon. We were greeted and politely invited to come back after the service was over. My enthusiasm from the service was in looking forward to the next time he would come over for a woodworking session. There were many questions going through my mind.

Cy came across the street to my attic shop after a Session meeting later in the week. He greeted me and said, "it is good to see that you are still alive after attending a Presbyterian Church service." I told him that it was somewhat of a surprise to me that I survived, but my Methodist relatives would be in a state of shock if they learned how badly I had sinned.

After our usual crude-joke greetings, we fixed a lamp he brought. Our evening 'bull session' started earlier than usual by me asking Cy what he really meant by saying *" as written by man."* Our Methodist preacher never added those words. The evening extended into the wee-hours of the morning. That night was the first time in my life that I really understood the effect that a minister of the gospel can have on another person. Cy's easy going and non-pushy manner had finally led his hard-nosed, woodworking, sinner neighbor to have complete trust and confidence in a 'man of the cloth.'

I believed that God had worked in my life during the war. Why He did so was beyond my reasoning capabilities. Cy did not try to be a big-shot preacher and give me answers to the questions of how or why God acted as He did. In his calm and humble manner he said, "I cannot tell you why God acts as He does; only God can lead you to the answers of the questions you ask. As a pastor, I try to live by the Christian theology taught in seminary, but fail every day of my life. It might be just a little thought going through my brain that is more negative than it should be, however, that is a failure on my part."

He went on to explain that human beings had written all of the words in the Bible. "God did not write those words, so why would any pastor say unequivocally, *this is the Word of God?* That is misleading his congregation. Scribes and bishops make mistakes when writing and copying text. God does not make mistakes. Biblical scholars know there are errors, myths, discrepancies, and total disagreement on some subjects in the Holy Bible. That does not mean that Biblical teachings are wrong. It only means that scribes and authors are human and did make mistakes. In some instances it is quite obvious that different documents were being used for reference when attempting to tell the same story. The Bible could be more meaningful to many people if pastors would only admit that men wrote every word and men do make mistakes in writing, copying, and translating text. As a pastor, I believe Biblical philosophy is strengthened, not diminished, when non-seminarians are told the truth about the Bible."

Cy then asked if I knew about the Vinegar Bible. "No, I never heard of a Vinegar Bible," was my answer. He went on to explain that in Kent County, England there is a town by the name of Chiddingstone. In their small church a Bible on a stand is always open, which has the word vinegar mistakenly written for vineyard. The scribe copying text got careless or tired and wrote the word vinegar instead of vineyard. I told Cy the scribe might have indulged in spirits of applejack while copying Biblical text instead of the Holy Spirit as taught in the Bible. Cy came from Erie County grape country and didn't know that in Clarion County farmers made applejack instead of wine. Grapes do not grow well in Beaver Township, but apples are abundant. Applejack is a brandy distilled from hard cider and much better and more potent than wine. Cy did not appear to be too interested in the virtues of applejack as compared to wine and went on with the following comments.

"Kenton, I want to make some comments, which come from a person who found the Lord, went to seminary, was ordained, and is desperately trying to live and do my work according to the teachings in the Bible." Cy's words may not be verbatim, but his little sermon has been remembered.

"When you find the One who can answer all of your questions and explain everything in the Bible then you will know that you have met God. No human being can do that for you. You cannot 'Hurry Up Son' and find Truth on anyone's schedule except what He has planned for you. You faced death and believe that God interceded for you. Always be aware of your spiritual experience up there in the sky on a B-24 Bomber during the war. His spirit is always with you and with all things at all times. God's schedule for you may require a lifetime to discover Divine Truth, rather than a sudden conversion. Someday, you will learn that the Christ has always been within you, which is the secret of Divine Truth and Christianity."

Cy's few sentences in the attic woodshop, covered with sawdust, had more meaning for me than any other sermon in my life. I did not understand what he meant by saying, *"Christ has always been within you."* Rather than act like I understood him, my reaction was stupid by not having Cy explain what that meant. The words cannot be written as eloquently as the pastor of a rural church spoke them. However, his message came through loud and clear to me and has been an inspiration in my life.

- Seek answers on your own.
- Preachers do not have all of the answers.
- Have faith in God.
- Be aware of spiritual experiences.
- God's spirit is in all things, at all times.
- Salvation cannot be rushed.
- You cannot 'Hurry Up Son' to find the Lord.
- Truth may require a lifetime.
- Men not God wrote the Holy Bible.
- God is infallible; humans make mistakes.
- The Truth you are seeking is within you.

Awareness, is the best description of my reaction to the words of a gentle and kind man. Perhaps Cy knew that he was planting seeds that may take many years to germinate. I wish he were alive to ask that question. Cy probably understood me better than I ever understood myself.

If Pastor Moorhead would have taken a typical preacher approach and asked me to kneel and pray with him to seek Jesus my reaction would have been to throw him out of my woodshop. Empathy can have a profound effect on another person's life. I now believe that Cy Moorhead knew exactly what he was doing in his profession. Unfortunately, the professional work is more difficult and takes a lot longer when they encounter sinners like me.

Later, in thinking about Cy's words I realized that he had never mentioned the name Jesus. Perhaps he thought I may freak-out due to my 'Hurry Up Son' experience if he mentioned any name but God. My urge is to pick up the telephone and call Cy about his little sermon in my attic shop. There are many other questions I would like to ask those who are now deceased. Many of us wait too long to ask difficult questions from those that may have the wisdom to guide us in the quest for Truth.

Some weeks later, Cy gave me a poem that he thought was appropriate for my interest in clocks. Since that time, *The Clock of Life* has been glued on the inside of most clock cases made in my shop.

The Clock of Life

The clock of life is wound but once
And no one has the power
To know when the hands will stop
At an early or late hour.

NOW! Is the only time you have
Live, love, work with a will
Put very little faith in tomorrow
Your hands may then be still.

The little poem makes one wonder if we actually do understand what life is all about. There was a program on television stating that scientists accurately weighed a person's body just prior to death and immediately following death. To everyone's amazement the body weighed exactly the same at both times. What is life? Where did it go? Even the air that we cannot see can be measured in weight. If life has no weight then how can it be measured?

The more I concentrate on the question, *'What is life?'* the more convinced I am that God has mysteries HE does not intend to share with any human being, even preachers. LIFE--the single most important factor to every human being cannot be measured by weight. How can it be measured? Theologians are convinced they know where life goes after all bodily functions cease and we enter a state called death. Do they really know what happens to that elusive factor called life? Is it possible that nothing happens? To my knowledge there has never been one conclusive scientific experiment that proves this thing called 'life' goes anywhere after bodily functions cease.

Mentally, I can hear some relatives and others scream if they take time to read these words. So-called Christians and Theologians may say, "You are a nut." "You are an atheist." "Don't you believe in the Bible?" "Where are your parents and deceased loved ones?" "Why are you a church member?" "Do you not believe in Jesus Christ?" Their list of comments, questions, and criticism could probably fill many written pages.

Likewise, my list of unanswered questions is quite long. If Reverend McCaskey and his wife could magically come back to life they would probably whisper words in that boy's ear of 1933 something like, "hurry up old man. Your time on earth is fast running out. Others have professed they found Jesus Christ and are living normal lives." No thanks! Like Ron and Jack that didn't make the Teen Boys Class, too many people that I know who say they found Jesus Christ would never be admitted within my circle of friends. Several pastors and even one Rabbi I knew abdicated their theology commitment and now live with the wife of a former member of their congregation. What happened in their minds to, *"Thou shall not covet?"* Many people in their families would have experienced fewer traumas if the preachers had practiced what 'Saint' Victor Botts taught us in the Teen Boys Class, "When you get aflame with sexual passion for a female you have no right to covet then go and masturbate. If I ever learn you defiled a female then I will personally choke the crap out of you."

Perhaps my father was correct and his son is one of those people that need proven facts to believe anything. Engineering standards and mathematics have served well during a lifetime consisting of a diverse engineering and business career. They have not served well in attempting to find redemption. Redemption as defined in theology meaning, "Salvation from sin through Jesus' sacrifice."[1] That boy at the altar in 1933 is still struggling today to find what the preacher and his wife convinced the others in the communicant class they had found. Personal comparison is a dangerous pursuit; however, that boy did exceedingly well in his choice of a wife and a business career over fifty years. Their marriage resulted in two outstanding children and seven extraordinary grandchildren. Sometimes, it seems that eleven-year old boy was blessed to tell the truth and admit he did not find Jesus Christ that night in April 1933. When compared to the lives of others that were in the communicant class and answered *yes* to the preacher's question he has been blessed.

Was Vic Botts correct to infer we had 'turkey brains' and they never

---

[1] *American Heritage Dictionary*, 3rd edition, Microsoft Bookshelf

developed further? Cy Moorehead's sermonette is more comforting.

"You cannot 'Hurry Up Son' and find the Lord on anyone's schedule except what He has scheduled for you. God's schedule for you may require an entire lifetime to achieve Truth, rather than a sudden conversion."

God's plan for some people may require a lifetime to achieve Truth. If you are one of those people that would be known as 'God's-lifers' (requiring a lifetime for Truth) then the Christian Church requires you to be less than completely honest about your beliefs, or knowledge, in order to qualify for membership. 'YES' is the only acceptable answer for church membership to the question: Do you believe in Jesus Christ, God's only son, born of the Virgin Mary and was crucified_ _ _ _? The Christian Church has created many dichotomous individuals. People will say they believe something in order to gain church membership, but like Victor Bott's Teen Boys class they aren't sure what they believe. Too many times church members made statements like the following when I was active in church work:

- The virgin birth is just a fable.
- I believe in Christianity but not the resurrection.
- Angels are a myth.
- Easter is a nice holiday; did it really happen that way?
- Where has Jesus been for over two thousand years?
- I have Bibles but never read them.
- The Bible is too confusing for me to understand.
- Many things in the Bible do not agree; what am I to believe?
- How can the preacher believe all this stuff he talks about?
- Heaven and Hell sound like fantasylands to me.
- Why can Christians only be admitted into Heaven?
- Where do non-Christians go when they die?
- Does the preacher know more than me if it's all in the Bible?
- Don't tell the preacher I can't believe some of his sermons.
- Why is there no historical record of Jesus?
- Did god actually speak directly to the prophets?

During four terms as a Presbyterian Elder and six years as Sunday school Superintendent and teacher, people asked me such weird questions that you wondered why they bothered to get up on Sunday morning. Probably they felt more comfortable asking an active layman questions than to risk embarrassment by asking the preacher. The problem was, as a layman I did not have the correct answer to their questions. Often times I wondered if the preacher's answer was correct to questions asked when interceding for others on a no-name basis. Some of his answers seemed rather vague. It was a rare opportunity for a layman! As the vice president and general manager of the largest employer in town (over 2,000 employees) it became quite apparent that many people were more at ease to ask me questions they would never dare to ask the preacher. Also, there was a church-related association with the boss that would never be available during working hours at the office, manufacturing plants, or engineering building due to time constraints.

My active participation in the Rocky Grove Presbyterian Church started just prior to Reverend Cyrus Moorhead answering a call to serve in a church close to where he was raised. I always regretted that he was not there to help me with answers to questions people asked. Cy knew that I had never experienced a sudden conversion and could not in complete honesty say that I had received Jesus Christ as my Lord and Savior. He convinced me that by participating in church work it may lead me to that mystical experience of finding Jesus Christ that eluded me since 1933.

After our daughter Elaine was born we later spent a lot of time as a family of four working in the church. At Christmas, it was fun for Kent and Elaine to help Florence and me measure out candy to put in boxes for each child at Sunday school. We all agreed that was the 'sweetest' part of being the Sunday school superintendent.

Cy Moorhead's successor, Reverend Calvin Wimer, had a heart attack shortly after coming to Rocky Grove. The elders agreed to fill-in while he recuperated. As laymen we worked very hard and actually increased both church membership and attendance. Wimer let it be known that he was most unhappy with our performance after returning to active duty.

We were proud of how church membership and Sunday attendance had increased. Over 300 people were regularly attending Sunday school and over 200 the church service, which was a dramatic increase. However, the preacher resented it! Why, I will never know. I do know that his negative attitude caused we church elders to become very uncomfortable about our work. To be chastised by a preacher for increasing Sunday school attendance while at the same time, being the head of the largest employer in town was an irritation and complete dichotomy for me. At the company our managers worked toward pre-defined goals. The preacher's goals were inconsistent with Biblical teachings, *"Go throughout the whole world and preach the gospel to all men."*[1] Perhaps my brains should have been left out in the parking lot instead of trying to find Jesus Christ through being a church elder and Sunday school superintendent.

---

[1] Mark 16:15 (Today's English Version)

The hard lesson learned was that it is dangerous for a layman to ever tread on the preacher's turf, or to attempt to use your brain within a Christian church if it has anything to do with Bible interpretation. Seminarians, not laymen, are the only ones authorized within the Christian hierarchy to interpret the Bible. Some do a very poor job and deserve to have the vacant pews in their church.

What I learned as an active layman was significant. Nearly everyone in our church was going through the same mental anguish about Christianity and the divinity of Jesus Christ that I was as a church elder. It was the most empathetic experience of my entire life. Fortunately, there was always the comfort of reverting to the 'party-line' of the church, namely FAITH. When all else fails to satisfy the layman's questions then the fallback position of Christianity is, you must have faith and never question such things. It is too bad that such a position will not work with a corporate board of directors.

The head of a large organization never wants to be wrong or admit that he doesn't have or cannot get correct answers to employee's questions. When the questions pertain to religion then it puts the elder/church school superintendent/manager in a position similar to what the legal profession refers to as double jeopardy. It quickly became evident to me that the senior manager of a large organization, concerned about his employees, should never take an active role in a church that is attended by many of those employees. The manager may be producing outstanding results for his board of directors and stockholders. He can never give employees precise answers to questions about Christianity, because, a faith-based religion introduces an elusive factor that is not acceptable in his business-management style, namely **FAITH.**

The inventors of Christianity were true geniuses to come up with the requirement that a person must rely upon faith alone when there are no definitive answers to troubling questions. The American Heritage® Dictionary of the English Language, 1996 edition, defines **Faith** (Theology), "The theological virtue defined as secure belief in God and a trusting acceptance of God's will." In Hebrews 11: 1 (Revised Standard Version) we are taught that, *"Now faith is the assurance of things hoped for, the conviction of things not seen."* Both definitions contain an elusive unknown factor that is troubling to many laymen. In fact, preachers and church lay people can make some of us feel really stupid by inferring their faith is stronger than yours. That boy kneeling at the altar in 1933 at the Knox, PA Methodist Church was certainly made to feet stupid just because he could not hurry up and find Jesus Christ that night.

Does anyone have the correct answers? Why am I still struggling to learn what it is that people experience when they say they have found Jesus?

During the many years that I was an active church elder and Sunday school superintendent why did the Jesus experience elude me? The older I get the more convinced I become that it is not possible for me to receive theological redemption, which is salvation from sin through Jesus' sacrifice.

By making a diligent effort to fulfill my obligation to seek Truth it now makes me feel cheated by the church. Why doesn't the church do a better job of teaching and permit us to debate religious subjects instead of just saying you must have faith? My efforts to seek Truth have required the reading and studying of many books and to concentrate on the actual meaning of words in the Bible. Following are some of those subjects:

- History of Christianity.
- Inquisition of Roman Catholic Church.
- Medieval history.
- Attempt to find a historical Jesus.
- Origination of Baptism and Eucharist (communion).
- Origination of Christmas and Easter.
- Read many books by Bible scholars and theologians.
- Actual words in the Bible. Not theology.
- Ancient Mysteries, such as Isis/Osiris.
- Comparative religion.
- Non-canonical gospels such as Thomas and Philip.
- Dead Sea Scrolls.
- Nag Hammadi library.

That boy at the alter in 1933 is still trying to 'hurry up son and find the spirit of Jesus.' He is finally learning what it means to find the spirit of Jesus. It is not what the church teaches! Reverend Cyrus Moorhead told me that, "The Christ you are seeking is within you and God's spirit is within you and within all things at all times." If Cy was correct then I have been the problem by seeking an external source. If God's spirit and what I have been seeking are inherently within me then it becomes my sole obligation to redirect my efforts inwardly to find the Divine Truth. Christianity has not taught me how to do that.

Does the Church Cheat Laymen?

Like so many Christians, I now feel cheated by the Church. During most of my life I have accepted what the Christian church taught, believed the Bible to be the Word of God, and the pastor was always the authority on religious items. Recent studies now make me feel like being a 'religious ostrich' for many years. My head was hid in the sand with regard to stories in the Bible that couldn't possibly be true, which the church teaches as God's Word. FAITH-ful (*faithfool*) followers do not question sermons about turning the Nile River and all the water containers in Egypt into blood, parting the Red Sea so God's chosen people could escape, Adam and Eve discovering their nakedness, Jonah in the belly of a whale, God permitting himself to be killed in the likeness of Jesus, and on and on. Many faithful followers have also been like the second definition of an ostrich as defined in Microsoft Bookshelf 2000 Dictionary, "One who tries to avoid disagreeable situations by refusing to face them."

Scholars have known for many years about discoveries that I have learned through my personal effort in the search for Truth. It is a sad fact that few Christians know what scholars have learned about the many connections between Christianity and the Ancient Mystery religions. If so-called Faith is more important than facts, then many Christians may not care. They will continue to be deluded by the inability of the Church to teach the Truth. The faith versus fact scenario may well be the direct cause of the 'vacant pew syndrome' that so many preachers lament about.

In this technological age, lay people with questioning minds are learning about the myths and Biblical inconsistencies that scholars have known for many years, but presented as facts by the Church. When the Church teaches that myths are facts then young well-educated people become disillusioned. Also, older church members feel cheated when they learn that Church traditions and teachings they have revered from childhood are actually pre-Christian myths that were originally taught by allegory. The ancient mystical teaching allegories were known and accepted to be mythical presentations and not facts. Each allegory taught the initiate a separate lesson on how to improve their life during the training period.

Christianity claims to be the greatest story ever told. No argument can be made against that claim, provided the mythology is not presented as God-given dogma or creed that cannot be changed. People should attempt to live and follow the teachings of Jesus. Scholars now know that the teachings of Jesus came from very ancient mystical teachings and Egyptian theology, which is far more ancient than the Jesus era. Even the Talmud of Judaism states unequivocally that Jesus spent his early manhood in Egypt where He learned the *ancient magical mysteries.* What was the true mission of Jesus? Was it actually an attempt to teach the Jews the ancient mysteries? Many Biblical scholars think that was precisely His mission. However, they believe that Jesus abrogated his vows of secrecy and preached the secret mystical teachings to non-initiates. It would be impossible to understand the *ancient mysteries* without advancing through each level of teaching in the correct sequence.

To understand and become proficient in the *ancient mystery* allegorical teachings a candidate proceeded from the first through the final lesson. The candidate had to become proficient and approved by superiors at each level before proceeding to the next, or higher, level of teaching. Pythagoras spent 20 years in Egypt studying the ancient mystical wisdom to achieve teaching proficiency. He contributed to the development of mathematics and Western rational philosophy and influenced Plato and Aristotle. Due to tyrannical rule in Samos, Ionia Pythagoras went to Crotona in Southern Italy to start a school in 532 BCE He was born in c. 580 and died c. 500 BCE.[1] It seems odd that the births, deaths, and writings of so many more ancient scholars are recorded, but there are no known records of anything pertaining directly to Jesus. Throughout the New Testament there are teachings, traditions, and words ascribed to Jesus, many years after His death, that came directly from the ancient mysteries such as Isis/Osiris, Ma'at, and Mithraism.

Egyptian religious philosophy (theology) was known as Ma'at. Well known Egyptian achievements in architecture, science, commerce, and peaceful living with one another and their government were a direct result of Ma'at. Egyptian hieroglyphics confirm, *"Ma'at has no one meaning, but includes truth, true, right, real, genuine, upright, righteous, just, steadfast, and unalterable. Ma'at has not been broken since the time of Osiris."*[2]

Many Bible scholars believe the Jews created a Jesus Myth, which also gave them a resurrected God/man. During that era all other countries and civilizations had a mythical Goddess/God-man religion taught by allegory. People knew the allegories were mythical and not facts. Characters and events were used to represent ideas or principles from human wisdom condensed and documented thousands of years prior to the Jesus era.

Recently, the Pope confirmed that the church has no documented facts pertaining to the date Jesus was born. He said December 25 was chosen because it has become a popular mid-winter holiday. The Pope's reference to the birthday of Jesus immediately hoisted red flags in the minds of Biblical scholars. Scholars and many laymen have known for centuries that December 25 was the day celebrated in ancient Rome and other places as the birthday of Mithras. The Vatican stands on the ground that once held the shrine dedicated to Mithras the Sun God, from which the Christian Halo originated.

---

[1] *Encyclopedia Britannica*
[2] Quote from transliterated hieroglyphics in *Egyptian Book of the Dead*, page cxix

The 'too little-too late' admission by the Pope was during my early research on Christian holidays. My only desire was to study the recorded history pertaining to major holidays and rituals observed by the Christian church. How did they evolve? Who ordained that we should celebrate Christmas, Virgin Birth, Good Friday, Easter, Baptism, Communion (Eucharist), etc. My desire has been to attain historical knowledge about each of those occasions. The Christian church teaches that you must not question the Bible, holy days, and rituals, but accept them purely on faith.

During WWII our crew had faith the B-24 Bomber would always return safely to the air base after dropping bombs on the target. We were highly trained to question the slightest deviation from the airplane being anything other than a reliable flying machine. If the power pack for an engines turbo super charger malfunctioned at high altitude the flight engineer had better forget about the Operation Manual, risk frostbite, rip off his flying gloves, and install the spare. Otherwise, an expensive aircraft and her crew were doomed. Flight crews believed God was protecting them; however, He gave us the right to make decisions and question flight manual procedures if our lives were in danger. 'Blind faith' and 'don't ask questions' were not acceptable.

Why should it be any more acceptable in the church when our salvation is at risk? Humans, not God, wrote every word in both the Bible and the B-24 (bible) Operation Manual. Humans do make mistakes! We were encouraged to question and challenge the written words in the Operation Manual. Why are we chastised as Christian laymen for asking questions about what the church claims is God's Operation Manual, the Holy Bible, when the Bible authors do not agree? They do not even agree upon such a basic church teachings as to whether Jesus was crucified on a cross or hung on a tree.[1]

It has never been my intent to challenge anyone's religious beliefs. In my judgment, a person will contribute far more to life by attending church and never asking questions, than to have no religious affiliations. By doing so they will make many preachers happy that do not have the answers for those difficult Biblical questions. Or perhaps preachers that do know the truthful answers but must follow the party line of the church or be unemployed. Something is wrong when intelligent people are required to not ask questions and refrain from seeking knowledge that is only the 'turf' of theologians. How can scientific and engineering minds be expected to abrogate the principals and knowledge they live by? Are they to put education aside and become literalists of the Bible? It is also disconcerting when intelligent lay-people get so caught up in the non-questioning syndrome of the Christian

---

[1] Acts 5:30 and Galatians 3:13 (Peter and St. Paul both say He was hung on a tree.)

church they refuse to have any discussions outside of the dogma and creed. They appear to shut down their otherwise intelligence when the Bible or Christianity is the center of conversation that may differ from what the Church teaches.

Too many times during my business career people have cheated and outright told lies when, at the same time, they wanted it to be known by everyone they were devout Christians. The Christian philosophy in the Bible does not appear to condone the actions of that type of person. One individual got so carried away with their Christianity they even made a trip to the Holy Land for the reason they said, "to be where it all happened." The individual's conduct after returning made it quite obvious that nothing extraordinary happened to them.

People that flaunt their religion are difficult for managers to handle in a business organization. It appears that 'religion flaunters' want to impress other employees and management, by giving the impression they have experienced something spiritual that has avoided others. During a discussion after one stockholder's meeting a Methodist minister told me that he describes a sanctimonious type person as, "wearing your religion on your sleeve, instead of having it in your heart where it belongs".

The minister was a stockholder and had advised me that one of my corporate officers should be counseled with, and told to tone-down his making sure that everyone knows he is a very religious person. The minister also told me it was his opinion that company officers should promote the business by daily applying Christian teachings in their responsibilities, rather than the reverse. Sometime later, I learned that particular officer would 'cheat the socks off you' if given an opportunity.

It makes one wonder why there are so many 'so-called' Christians that do not apply their Christianity in a more uniform manner, and why there are so many different Christian denominations, each claiming their creed to be the direct Word of God. If you believe that God is the same *yesterday, today, and forever'* would He not instruct all Christian denominations exactly the same? Perhaps periodic efficiency exams should be given to maintain membership in a church. That is probably not a good suggestion, as many churches now have too many vacant pews on Sunday morning.

Holidays –Rituals –Traditions

"A Patron Saint of Hemorrhoids! Come on now Chris, you have to be kidding." He said, "Kidding hell, we have a patron saint for just about everything; McElhattan you are too thickheaded to understand these simple everyday things of life." From that conversation the vision of my 'turkey brain' from Victor Botts Teen Boys Class immediately came to mind. Like Vic Botts, Chris was a diamond in the rough that could teach you a lot, provided you would listen.

That conversation went on several years ago during lunch with a Pennsylvania State Trooper and myself. The trooper was a good friend, a really fun guy, and an absolute non-questioning Roman Catholic that claimed to see the outline of Jesus or the Virgin Mary in the sun's reflection or even spilled gravy on the table. Some of his beliefs seemed completely beyond reality to me. It was always fun to meet him at a restaurant near our office. We never made dates to meet, but often agreed we looked forward to the other one being there at lunchtime. We were so opposite that we seemed to relate to each other for that reason. He was a classic looking policeman–big, raw boned, deep voice, wore his uniform well, and you knew immediately if he liked you or not.

Chris loved to intimidate people with his awesome size, immaculate uniform, sidearm in a holster, and a voice like a chainsaw ripping through logs. After a few minutes of intimidating a stranger the charm was turned on and you knew immediately that he had a big heart. Several times I took Chris to our office with the plan to let people know that State Troopers are not all bad guys. Before introducing him to people I would say, "Chris act normal and show them what an old bastard you really are and then turn on the charm to show them that State Troopers can be normal people." He played the role to perfection. My sobriquet for him was 'Chris' spelled with a 't' on the end. Lunches were not as interesting after Chris retired.

After returning from a church organized trip to Medjugorje, Yugoslavia (now Bosnia-Hercegovina) Chris was so excited about the association with priests and other Catholics that from then on I called him 'Chris' with capital 'T.' I told him the T stood for troublemaker and not to begin thinking that he was Christ. Young girls had experienced 'Our Lady's Apparitions' of the Virgin Mary several years prior to his trip. It was fascinating to learn about his visit to the apparition site near Medjugorje.

One day another State Trooper was leaving as I sat down with Chris for lunch. He said, "I'm going to pray to Saint Fiacre tonight for that trooper." "Why would you do that?" I asked, "we protestants pray to God." "Because, he gives me a pain in the buttocks and St. Fiacre is the Patron Saint of Hemorrhoids," he said. Of course, I thought he was just making up a tale. Upon researching Patron Saints it proved that Chris was correct. Saint Fiacre is the Patron Saint of Hemorrhoids.

Several later lunch conversations centered on Patron Saints. It was interesting and I learned more about Patron Saints than I really wanted to know. Chris was certainly correct in saying the Roman Catholic Church has a Patron Saint for just about anything that ails a person. If you have ulcers pray to Saint Borromeo, Patron Saint of Ulcers/Stomach Pains and celebrate his Feast Day on November 4. With a hangover you pray to Saint Viviana, Patron Saint of Hangovers and the Feast Day is December 2. Abused wives should pray to Saint Rita, Patron Saint of Wife Abuse with a May 22 Feast Day. Saint Guigole is the Patron Saint of Impotence with a March 3 Feast Day. Those with venereal disease or syphilis should pray to Saint George, Patron Saint of Syphilis. Can you visualize a group of people meeting in the church for an April 23 Feast Day to ask Saint George for relief from their sexual disease caused by copulating with an infected whore? I cannot! There are many more Patron Saints and even one for most countries. Mary of the Immaculate Conception is the Patron Saint of the United States with December 8 the Feast Day.

One day Chris was all smiles when I met him. He presented me with a Guardian Angel automobile visor clip. "Now what in the world am I to do with that thing? "I asked him. He told me to read what it says and then put it in my car. It reads; *PROTECT ME, MY PASSENGERS, AND ALL WHO PASS BY WITH A STEADY HAND, AND A WATCHFUL EYE.* "Chris, it doesn't say anything about being protected from crazy State Troopers like you," I told him. "KE, I'm telling you the gospel truth when I say that about 85% of the Pennsylvania State Troopers are genuine angels. We try to be courteous with motorists and kind to everyone that we have any association with. The other 15% are genuine bastards and delight in giving people a hard time. I pray to Saint Fiacre every night for that bunch," he said.

Protestant Christianity claims some things to be true that seem weird. The Roman Catholicism education from trooper Chris made my Protestant beliefs pale by comparison. It is no wonder that Martin Luther revolted against the Roman Church. Such items as a diaper from baby Jesus enshrined in a golden box at a cathedral in Aachen, Germany, which is only displayed every seven years. Boards from His crib in the manger are under lock and key and behind layers of glass at the Vatican. At Notre Dame Cathedral in France there is a Crown of Thorns without any thorns on it. The thorns were taken off the vine and individually given to churches and chapels in Europe for worship. The Church claims the Crown Of Thorns worn by Jesus was miraculously found around 600 C.E. in the Holy Sepulcher. There are so many single thorn confirmations from the crown that one vine could not possibly have that many thorns. Botanists named the plant *Zizyphus spina-christi* in honor of Christ. It is difficult to believe these items are authentic when dates for the birth and death of Jesus are not known.

Chris was a rare opportunity for me to get some insight into the mind of a person that was raised in the beliefs of the Roman Catholic Church. He would discuss any subject and told me that items like the diaper, boards, and thorns are what the church officially class as Relics. His favorite Roman Catholic Statue is in a church at Brest, France. The Statue is Saint Guignole, Patron Saint of Impotence, which depicts a nude saint with an erect penis. Chris claims that women stand in awe as they observe the saint's manhood. My guess is that it's a carryover from the Phallus Worship Fertility Rite of ancient Greece. Whatever the reason for the statue it indicates the Christian Church will adopt most anything from the *ancient mysteries,* sanctify it, then claim it is a revelation from God.

As friends, we respected each other's beliefs and had genuine open discussions on many church related items. Thanks to a friend Chris with a 't' my interest was sparked about the historical roots of holidays, rituals, sacraments, traditions, and other church-sanctified things. He thought Protestant Christianity was being short-changed to have only two sacraments when the Roman Catholic Church has seven. At the time I did not have the courage to embarrass my friend by telling him that all seven sacraments of the Roman Catholic Church came directly from the ancient *Mysteries of Mithras,* which came from a more ancient source.

The Roman Catholic Church has seven sacraments that were practiced in the worship of Mithras, God of the Sun.

1. Communion
2. Baptism
3. Confirmation
4. Penance
5. Extreme Unction
6. Ordination
7. Matrimony

Protestant Christianity evolved from the Ninety-Five Theses, 'for the purpose of eliciting truth,' developed by Martin Luther. Luther was a priest that married a nun and denounced many teachings ordered from the Papacy in Rome. On October 31, 1517, the eve of All Saints Day, he fastened them on the door of the All Saints Church at Wittenberg, Germany. Since that time, most protestant denominations have retained only two of the original seven sacraments, which are Communion and Baptism.

Communion (Eucharist)

Cannibalism is repulsive to even think about. For your ancient ancestors it was a common practice. Eating human flesh mysteriously transformed the strength or wisdom from the deceased to the person eating human meat. Theology defines it as Transubstantiation; the doctrine holding that the bread and wine of the Eucharist are transformed into the body and blood of Jesus, although their appearances remain the same.[1] Regardless of what the preacher or priest may tell you the practice originated from cannibalism. It did not originate from The Last Supper of Jesus as taught in the Christian Church. Like so many rituals, Communion was 'borrowed' by the church from the *ancient mysteries* and Egyptian theology[2], sanctified, and from then on taught as originating from The Last Supper of Jesus Christ.

Anthropologists know that even current day tribes living along the Orinoco River that borders Venezuela-Colombia ceremonially eat meat from a deceased person to have the strength or wisdom of the departed one transferred to them. Human blood is consumed for the same reason. Jews and Romans thought the ritual of Communion was so obnoxious that they called the early Christians cannibals. In more civilized countries such as Egypt and Greece the ritual evolved to use wine and bread instead of violating a corpse. Records confirm that the practice of communion is far more ancient than what the church teaches about The Last Supper. In fact, it pre-dates the written records of the human race.

In Pagan worship the participant in the *Mysteries of Mithras* was given a consecrated wafer with the sign of the cross on it and the symbolic representation of Mithras saying,

"He who will not eat of my body and drink of my blood, so that he will be made one with me and I with him, the same shall not know salvation."

Many centuries later in the Gospel of John it is written that Jesus says,

"Unless you eat of the flesh of the Son of Man and drink his blood, you have not life in yourselves. Whoever eats my flesh and drinks my blood will live in me and I in him."

---

[1] Microsoft Bookshelf 2000
[2] See *Egyptian Book of the Dead,* transliteration & translation by E.A.W. Budge 1895, Dover Pub. 1967.

In the litigious society of today's world, the writer of the Gospel of John would find himself in a court of law charged with plagiarism.

Of course, educated people of today know that eating bread and drinking grape juice (wine) cannot possibly, through some magical process (transubstantiation), give a participant the strength and wisdom of a deceased person. Communion as practiced in the Presbyterian Church is a solemn and uplifting ritual. Who knows what actually goes on within the mind of the participants? For me, it is a ritual for taking time to reflect upon the teachings accredited to Jesus and ask myself, "how am I doing with regard to His teachings?" Invariably the answer is, "not too good!" For that reason alone, Communion is a good sacrament. It can make you think and reflect upon your actions in daily life, and hopefully try to improve yourself. Probably none of us do enough of that.

Baptism

Life depends upon water. Oannes was the god of water in ancient Sumer. It is interesting to follow that name through the translations of Greek, Latin, Hebrew, and to English when the name becomes John. Who was John the Baptist? Where did he learn the ritual of baptism? My Bibles or pastors do not answer those questions satisfactorily. In the ancient *Hymn To Dementer,* by Homer, the 'ritual purity' is the condition of salvation and people must be baptized to wash away their previous sins.

The ritual of baptism by water is so ancient that it can be found in virtually all of the ancient mystery rites. In some rituals of anointing with water it appears to have been a community undertaking for young people to become members. The ritual was supposed to be a visible indication of an inward cleansing or spiritual renewal.

In Egypt people participating in the Isis/Osiris ritual were required to publicly confess and repent their sins to a priest before being permitted to participate in baptism inside the Isis temple. John the Baptist preached a baptism of repentance for the forgiveness of sins.[1] Only in the Gospel of Luke is there an account of the birth of John the Baptist.[2] Scholars believe the writer of Luke worked from the Gospel of Mark, but why is the birth of John ignored in Mark? In the third chapter of Luke verses 7 through 22 it gives an

---

[1] Luke 3:3

[2] Luke Chapter 1

account of John baptizing the multitudes. He starts out by saying, *"You brood of vipers. Who warned you to flee from the wrath and come?"*

Then John goes on to tell them what to do, such as tax collectors should collect no more than what is appointed. Soldiers should rob no one by violence and be content with their wages. If you have two coats share it with a person that has none and do likewise with food. All of the writings in Luke about baptism sound suspiciously like the Egyptian Isis/Osiris baptism along the Nile. John is the priest who conducts the baptism of repentance for the forgiveness of sins for the multitudes. Luke goes on to state in 3:21; *"Now when all the people were baptized, and when Jesus also had been baptized."*

Why did the sinless Son of God need to have his sins washed away by baptism? That is a very troubling question. The Christian Church and ordained ministers of the church simply cannot answer the question by quoting from the Bible. Also, the pastor saying that Jesus was showing the multitudes a good example by submitting to John's baptism does not answer the question correctly. None of my Bibles have any reference, whatsoever, of Jesus ever intending to be a good example by submitting to the 'baptism of repentance for the forgiveness of sins' as taught by John. It is pure and simple speculation, or hopeful wishing, on the part of anyone to state what the intentions of Jesus, or God, might have been. When you are told that everything you need to know about God is in the Bible always remember that men wrote those words, not God. There are profound things to learn about God that can never be reduced to written words on paper.

Why can't Christianity 'come clean' and explain to us laymen that baptism is a harmless ritual that preceded Christianity by thousands of years? Why does the Christian Church claim that a child is born in sin and cannot enter the gates of heaven unless baptized? Why does the Mormon Church search genealogy records for deceased people in other faiths that did not believe in baptism then ritually baptize their name and claim them to be on the Mormon roles in Heaven? Jews asked the Mormon Church to stop that practice and quit baptizing deceased Jews. Some things associated with religion seem rather bizarre!

The Dead Sea Scrolls were discovered in 1947. It was over twenty years later before the church-controlled interpretations were released for lay people to study. In the scroll text known as Community Rule it states, *"He shall be cleansed from all his sins by the spirit of holiness uniting him to its truth, his flesh is sprinkled with purifying water and sanctified by cleansing water, it shall be made clean by the humble submission of his soul to all the precepts of God."*

Initially, when the Church adopted the ritual of baptism from the Ancient Mysteries only adults were baptized. Later in the Fourth Century, St. Augustine took a very hard position on baptism. He went so far as to say, "Those unfortunate children who die without baptism must face the judgment of God. They are vessels of contumely, vessels of wrath, and the wrath of God is upon them. Baptism is the only thing that can deliver these unfortunate infants from the kingdom of death and the power of the devil. If no one frees them from the grasp of the devil, what wonder is it that they must suffer in the flames with him."[1]

The Church agreed with the theology of Augustine for the next five hundred years. Peter Abelard came up with the brilliant idea to create an intermediate heaven for unbaptized children in around 1100 C.E. A suburb of heaven was created (Limbus Infatum) where children that were not baptized would spend eternity. Their punishment was to suffer the grief of separation from the Lord (darkness) because of unclean souls. Later the Church created a Father's Limbo (Limbus Patrum) for the Old Testament saints and worthy pagans such as Plato, Aristotle, and Socrates. Baptism is just another of the many rituals the Church borrowed from the Ancient Mysteries and applied 'creative theology' to suit their needs, then claim it was original with Christianity. To tell young people their unbaptized dead child will never enter heaven is cruel theology.

The Church created the various levels of heaven, so apparently it is within their authority to say who can or cannot enter those fantasylands to spend eternity. Pennsylvania has over 140 religious denominations according to a recent Pittsburgh Post-Gazette article. Each denomination has its own peculiar beliefs about the sacrament of baptism. Of course, each is presented as the true Word of God as revealed to them, which makes all others wrong in their beliefs about baptism. If you cannot enter heaven in one denomination, then just shop around until you find one that suits your individual situation.

When our children were baptized the oath was taken to raise them in a Christian home and nurture their spiritual needs as the pastor dipped his hand in water and placed it on the child's head. It was a memorable day to stand at the altar and take that oath in the presence of grandparents, relatives, and the congregation. We always tried to raise them according to that simple oath. Probably we would have tried just as hard had we never taken the baptismal oath. Our parents raised us to believe that both mother and father must assume all responsibility for their children until they became adults!

---

[1] *Sacred Origins of Profound Things*, by C. Panati, Penguin Books 1996

Other Sacraments and Ceremonies

The Catholic Church has five other sacraments in addition to the two recognized by most protestant denominations as follows:

PENANCE makes amends or atones for one's sins.

EXTREME UNCTION prepares the soul for immediate entry into heaven by overcoming the temptations of the last hours of life. Recently a Catholic priest at St. Bernard's Church in Mt. Lebanon, PA told me that modern day priests do not like the term, because only God knows when a person's life will end here on earth. He said that most priests now practice the same ceremony for all sick people when a prayer is offered for their recovery and well being whether here on earth or in heaven.

CONFIRMATION helps children keep the faith. They are to defend it with martyrdom if required.

HOLY ORDERS help the priest honor his vow of chastity, perform divine worship, and administer the sacraments to his flock.

MATRIMONY aids the husband and wife in being faithful to each other, conceive children, and overcome the temptation of birth control. Civil marriages are discouraged in Catholicism, because the couple does not receive the spiritual support of the sacramental grace to help them in married life.

The terms used when a couple take the vows to become husband and wife are interesting. Matrimony as a sacrament derives from the Latin word 'mater', which means mother and shifts the emphasis to the female. Marriage derives from the Latin word 'maritare', which means to become a husband. Therefore, matrimony is feminine and marriage is masculine. A church wedding puts emphasis upon the female and a secular wedding upon the male. Some societies require a verification of copulation to complete the wedding ceremony when the male and female mythically become as one.

In Judaism a child is considered a Jew if the mother is Jewish. It makes no difference what religion the father practices. At age thirteen a Jewish boy is recognized as an adult through the ceremony of Bar Mitzvah, which means 'son of the commandment.' A Jewish girl reaches the age of moral reason at age twelve through the ceremony of Bat Mitzvah, meaning 'daughter of the commandment.' The ceremonies are impressive. Early in the nineteen hundreds the Society for the Advancement of Judaism promoted the Bat Mitzvah for girls to encourage equality between the sexes.

There was a belief in ancient Judaism that, 'a man is not a man until united with a woman, and a man with no wife is not a complete human being.' Some scholars believe that if Jesus was not a married man then His story is a myth, because in Judaism at that time it was considered an awful sin to not be married and produce children. A single male adult of marriageable age that was not married was ridiculed and to be avoided. He was not true to Judaism. At times, Jews stoned an unmarried male to death and then hung him on a tree as an example for others to observe and avoid a similar fate. Of course, that may have been for homosexuality, which Jews abhorred. (Leviticus 18:22)

What did Peter and St. Paul actually mean when they wrote that Jesus was hung on a tree? (See page 41) Acts 5:30 and Galatians 3:13 are extremely troubling. They are verses that some theologians would like to eliminate from the Bible. Did you ever hear a minister refer to those verses in a sermon or study sessions? Of course not, they simply do not have an explanation as to why Peter and Paul both say that Jesus was hung on a tree. It is just another of the many problems created for Christianity when the gospel writings do not agree. When lay people read the Bible seriously and compare passages of scripture, the inconsistencies will give them the shock of their life if they have previously been non-questioning literalists.

Lucifer/Satan

The Roman Catholic Church readily admits humans created the various levels of heaven to make an eternal mythical place for children and pious adults that were not baptized. The church says to forget the facts it is only faith that counts. If we, the Church, want to create several heavens then it is up to our faithful flock to believe they exist. How then was Hell created? When people do not use their God-given brain to ask questions or do research to seek the truth they can be mislead by the Bible. One example is the Latin name of Lucifer.

The book, *Life Lines*, by Dr. R. Leslie Holmes, published in 2000, refers to the name Lucifer on page 26. It is an excellent book for those in search of Divine Truth. The reference to Lucifer explains how self-worship made a devil out of an angel. Supposedly the angel Lucifer became the devil. When reading those words in *Life Lines* it brought to mind Latin words that had been recently studied. The Bible reference is to Isaiah 14:12-14. There are two problems created by using the name Lucifer, whether in the King James Bible version or as a canonical reference to confirm there is a Satan or Hell.

1.   Lucifer is a Latin name. The Roman Latin language did not exist at the time that name was written in Isaiah. Latin was developed many centuries after the time of Isaiah. The name Lucifer in Latin derives from *lucem ferre*, which means 'bringer, or the bearer of light.' Isaiah's story is about the fallen Babylonian

King Sennacherib and has nothing to do with Satan. The expression used in the Hebrew text is *Helal*, son of *Shahar*, which translates as 'Day star, or son of the Dawn.' Lucifer was the name given to the morning star (Venus) by the Roman astronomers. Venus appears in the sky just before dawn in that part of the world.

2.　　The King James 1611 Authorized Version of the Bible is simply incorrect. Scholars authorized by the Catholic King James I to translate the Bible into English did not use the Hebrew texts. Instead they used the Catholic Vulgate Bible produced by St. Jerome in the fourth century. Jerome mistranslated the Hebrew metaphor, 'Day star, son of the Dawn' as Lucifer. Apparently the Church and Bible writers of that period were so anxious to establish Biblical verification for a Satan and Hell that they purposely misused the Latin word Lucifer. Over the centuries the Latin word Lucifer for morning star became the disobedient angel ejected from heaven to rule in Hell eternally. Lucifer became synonymous with Satan, the Devil, and the Prince of Darkness in Christian tradition instead of the true meaning of 'morning star', which Isaiah had also used. The creation of a Satan and Hell gave the church another opportunity to create a fear factor for increased power over the people.

Fortunately, biblical scholars of all faiths have recognized for many years there are mistranslations and misunderstandings from using words that the translation is lost or evolved into different meanings. To correct the problem a conference was called in 1946 to translate the Bible from the original sources. This massive effort resulted in the *New Testament of The New English Bible* being published in 1961. The Old Testament was published nine years later. Translators from all denominations reviewed every verse and word in the Bible. Rightly so, the name 'Lucifer' was stricken from all the revised versions. In my New International Version of the Bible the words of Isaiah in Chapter 14, Verse 12 read:

> *"How have you fallen from heaven,*
> *O morning star, son of the dawn!*
> *You have been cast down to the earth,*
> *You who once laid low the nations!"*

How can those words be construed to confirm there is a Satan or Hell? Isaiah was writing about the fall from power of a notorious King. Sannacherib may have been an evil king but so were many other monarchs in history. To create the Christian dogma of Satan, the Devil, and Hell on that Bible verse seems rather ridiculous once the truth is known and understood.

This is another example of the Catholic Church teaching untruths as dogma for centuries, which laymen and seminarians are taught as the gospel truth. As an experiment, ten people were asked to explain, *who was Lucifer?* Ten people stated that Lucifer is another name for Satan or the Devil. Several of them were very emphatic that the Bible cannot be wrong. The Church has batted 1,000% on the deception of the name Lucifer.

Recently, I was given a presentation copy of the King James Bible. It still uses the name 'Lucifer' in the above verse in the place of 'morning star.' Why would any church continue to use text from a Bible that has been proven to be incorrect by all denominations? Is it because the words best support the point they are trying to make? Do they believe that no Bible can be wrong? Also, why do printing houses and publishers continue to print and sell Bibles that are totally misleading and all denominations agree they are incorrect? A handbook for salvation, the Bible, should be brutally accurate! Money is probably the incentive for publishing incorrect documents.

Christmas

What the Pope did not confirm (page 40) is that many virgin births were written about in ancient history and that Christianity parallels Mithraism. The Pagan religion of Mithraism threatened the very existence of Christianity in the Roman Empire. The Church officials were desperate to curtail the popularity of celebrating the birth of Mithras known as the Sun god. Their solution was true genius. No one knew when the birthday of Jesus was, if ever, so they conveniently declared it to be on December 25 the popular day for celebrating the Sun God's birthday.

One theologian went so far as to write, "we hold this day to be holy, not like the pagans because of the birth of the sun, but because of him that made it." It was a case of common objectives becoming very popular among the masses. From that day in the early three hundreds forward, December 25 became the official Church dogma for the birth of Jesus. In 1223 St. Francis of Assisi made wooden figures to depict Mary, Joseph, baby Jesus, sheep, and sheppards that he called the crèche. The name comes from the Old French word cresche, which means crib. In Latin, *adventis* means coming or look forward to. Advent is the English name and is now celebrated on the Sunday nearest to November 30. Advent now competes with Christmas shopping instead of fasting and prayer as was originally intended. Partying or shopping is more fun than to observe the dispirited celebration of the Church.

There have certainly been a lot of virgins that mythically got pregnant during the history of mankind. In fact, Mary the mother of Jesus was a latecomer in the long line of virgin births. If you believe all the virgin birth tales then one must conclude that God was a busy fellow impregnating all of those virgins through the years. Following are some of the more recognizable names that were miraculously born of a virgin:

1500 BC - Zoroaster born in Persia.

1200 BC - Krishna a Hindu.

700 BC - Indra born in Tibet.

650 BC - Mithras born in Syria

600 BC - Gautama Buddha born in India.

200 BC - Attis born in Phrygia.

There were many more sons of Virgins recorded through the years. They were all saviors to mankind and suffered similar fates. The story attributed to Jesus is as ancient as the writings of mankind. It has been written many times in various cultures.

The story of Mithras is an exact parallel to Jesus' story and very troubling to the Christian church. A pastor told me that some things in Christianity were taken from the more ancient mysteries. What he would not admit is that the name Jesus can be substituted for Mithras and the only difference in the stories is the name. The doctrines of Mithraism include a savior god, born of a virgin in humble surroundings, died and rose again on the third day, a mediator between God and man, baptism, sacrificial meal, resurrection, last judgment, and a heaven and hell. How could Jesus, born over 600 years after Mithras, have lived a life that was exactly identical? Why are the doctrines and creeds of the Christian church the same as was practiced in Mithraism? The church has no satisfactory answers to the questions. When ministers have been questioned on the subject they invariably use the fallback position of the church, which is: *you must not question these things in the Bible and accept them on Faith.*

In ancient times the Winter Solstice was frightening. People feared the sun might not return, as the days got shorter. Elaborate rituals, including sacrifice, were created to appease the sun god. The rituals became an annual necessity. Originally the church celebrated the ritual on January 6. Later it was moved to December 25 as an attempt to eclipse the popular Mithras celebration. More recently the time between December 25 and January 6 was chosen by the church to celebrate Epiphany. Epiphany is the celebration of the manifestation of the divine nature of Jesus by the Magi. Maji or Magus was a member of the Zoroastrian priestly caste of the Medes and Persians. According to legend, Magi traveled to Bethlehem to pay homage to the infant

Jesus. Magi are defined as sorcerers or magicians. The Winter Solstice slowly retreats in time and will occur on December 22 in the year 2002.

An interesting problem with virgin births is in the Gospel of Luke pertaining to the miraculous pregnancy of Elizabeth, the mother of John. She was six months pregnant when Mary, a kinswoman, visited her according to Luke. We are told in Luke Chapter 1 that Gabriel, the angel in the days of Herod, King of Judea, told Zechariah, *"your wife Elizabeth will bear you a son."* In Elizabeth's sixth month of pregnancy Gabriel appeared before Mary and told her, *"Mary, you have found favor with God. And behold, you will conceive in your womb and bear a son, and you shall call him Jesus."* After learning this Mary went to visit Elizabeth.

The problem is that Luke tells us Gabriel notified Elizabeth and Mary in the days of Herod. According to Roman records Herod died in 4 BC. Later in Chapter 2, Luke writes that Joseph went to the city of Bethlehem to be enrolled with Mary, his betrothed, who was with child. The census for enrollment was from a decree of Caesar Augustus in the year 6 CE when Quirinius was governor of Syria. We are taught that Luke was a physician. Luke's medical school must not have taught him that normal pregnancy lasts nine months, not ten years!

Easter

Eastre (Easter) was the goddess of fertility. Her earthly symbol was the prolific rabbit. Ancient people practicing the mystery religions developed rituals and ceremonies for events important to their survival. If crops did not grow then entire societies could starve. The pagan celebration of spring (meaning of Eastre) became so popular that the Council of Nicaea issued the Easter Rule for the Christian church; *Easter will be celebrated on the first Sunday after the first full moon on or following the vernal equinox.* Astronomically, Easter cannot be earlier than March 22 or later than April 25. At the same Council the cross was adopted for the official symbol of Christianity. It was convenient action on the part of the Christian church bishops, because a cross was the symbol on the wafer used during the sacrament of Communion in Mithraism.

Closely associated with Easter was the celebration of May Day. When we were young children, our school always had a May 1 celebration around the May Pole. Dancers intertwined long colored streamers descending from the pole, until the pole was fully covered with a weaving pattern. Mothers would work for weeks to make special dresses for girls and costumes for the boys. Everyone would pay homage to the mythical King Ozark.

We never knew that our pleasant spring celebration was actually the Phallus Worship Fertility Rite from ancient Greece. People can get so carried away with the pageantry of the occasion that facts are not checked to determine why anyone would go through such antics. Our parents, school officials, and preachers would be chagrined to learn that all the kids in town were actually celebrating an erect penis to assure that the queen's fertility would produce a 'bumper crop.' It makes me feel rather silly to have participated in Phallic Worship as a child and never troubled myself until recently to ask the question, why? The holiest Christian day, Easter Sunday, is named for the goddess of sex Eastre and Solis the sun god.

Antis and Tammuz were Semitic fertility gods. Syria had Adonis as their fertility god. The passion plays for these gods could have the name replaced by Jesus, and Christians would detect no difference. An effigy of the corpse was tied to a sacred pine tree and adorned with flowers. The corpse was wrapped in linen and buried in a sepulcher and on the third day rose again. These mystery gods all ascended into heaven, which offered hope for salvation to the masses. Another peculiar coincidence is that early Christianity had the death of Jesus on March 25, which was also the day attributed to the death of Adonis from a much earlier time.

Christmas and Easter are fun celebrations for children and adults. Whether Santa Claus or the Easter Bunny is the center of the excitement the affairs do bring families together for fun and feasting. Around the time of puberty young people learn that Santa Claus and the Easter Bunny are mythical. The Christian church and many adults appear to be comfortable for a long time in the future to not acknowledge these holidays as Pagan Mythical Rituals.

Perhaps a discussion on Christian holidays that originated from ancient mythical stories and rituals should conclude by quoting Dr. Albert Schweitzer, the great humanitarian, physician, and theologian as written in a 1984 book by I. Wilson. Dr. Schweitzer won the 1952 Nobel Peace Prize. He wrote, "*There is nothing more negative than the results of the critical study of the life of Jesus. The Jesus of Nazareth who came forth publicly as the Messiah, who preached the ethic of the kingdom of God, who founded the kingdom of heaven upon earth, and died to give his work its final consecration, never had any existence. This image has been destroyed from without; it has fallen to pieces, cleft and disintegrated by concrete historical problems, which came to the surface one after another.*"

Crosses

The cross had a symbolic meaning since long before the time of recorded history. Ancient societies studied by anthropologists confirm the use of a cross for many different symbolic meanings. What may come as a surprise to modern day Christians is how recently the Latin cross has become known as a symbol for Christianity. Also, it is impossible to prove historically whether the New Testament writers meant that Jesus was crucified on a Latin-type cross or just hung on a tree, which was the Jewish custom at that time.

Following are several common crosses of over three hundred listed in various encyclopedias. They all have a fascinating history.

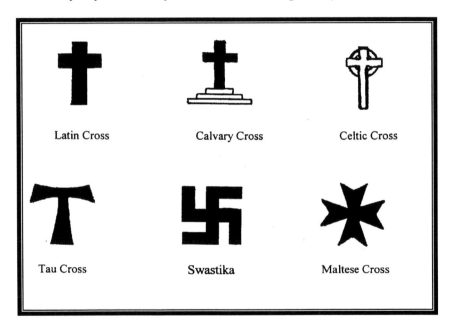

| Latin Cross | Calvary Cross | Celtic Cross |

| Tau Cross | Swastika | Maltese Cross |

Halo: The luminous ring surrounding the head or body of a sacred figure in Christianity originated in the Sol Invictus religion, which is Sun God worship. It is not classed as a cross, but people worship the figure within the halo. Halos are used so often in religious paintings that Christians need to know it pre-dates Christianity. An ancient statue and paintings of Isis holding her godson Horus (Sun God) always has a halo surrounding his head. It was used for the model in many paintings and statues of the Virgin Mary holding baby Jesus with a halo around his head.

Many crosses are significant only in heraldry. The Arms of McElhattan have a Greek or St. George cross (not shown) in red color on a shield, which makes four quadrants. The St. George cross is common on family arms in Scotland. It goes back to the time Crusaders were going to the Holy Land. Crusaders painted the cross on their shield then filled in the four quadrants with personal items of significance to their family. Saint George cross looks like a large plus (✚) sign similar to the Red Cross logo.

Latin Cross: Early Christians abhorred the symbolic use of the cross. Even today, the Sabbath-keeping Churches of God prohibit the symbolic use of the cross, because it is a pagan symbol. The use of the Latin cross is very ancient. The word cross derives from the Latin word *crux*, which means extension of the base. Crucifix is from the Latin word *crucifigere* and the word means to 'hang on a cross.' It was not until the reign of Constantine in the fourth century that the Latin cross was adopted as a symbol for Christianity. During the Nicene Convention men voted that Jesus would be known as a god and not a human. It took over 300 years to vote Jesus a god and adopt the cross symbol, which means *'savior'* in Egyptian hieroglyphics and derives to the words *Joshua* in Hebrew and *Jesus* in Greek.

Constantine's mother, Saint Helena 83 years old, went to Palestine and was guided by 'divine inspiration' to find the cross that was used for Jesus. Miraculously with the help of the Jews she found a wooden crucifix that was supposedly hidden under the Holy Sepulcher. Her son had a beautiful basilica built where the precious find was located. At least six major Christian cathedrals in Europe claim to have 'relics' from the original cross with the largest on display in the Vatican. If all of the cross relics were added together it would be impossible for an original cross to have been that large. The portion at the Vatican has been determined to be from a pine tree.

One significance of the Latin cross dates back to Greek mythology. They believed that Hyperborean was a race of people that lived in a perpetually warm and sunny land north of the source of the cold north wind. Hyperborean Celts had a triune religious system and believed that certain trees were sacred. Even Pliny writes about the cult of tree worship with the birch being sacred to northern shamans. The Celts worshipped the oak tree and cut it down for annual solstice fires to magically have the sun return. In Scotland the rowan tree is still revered as having magical powers. A small cross of rowan wood is tied to the tail of cattle for good luck. No Scottish ship would ever be launched without containing rowan wood. Soldiers from Scotland carry a small cross of rowan wood in their gear or on a string around their neck for good luck.

Ash and yew trees were revered in Ireland. The ancient Milesian alphabet Bobelloth consisted of only 18 letters and each represented a tree that was sacred. Animism has its basis as God emerging from a tree. The study of the Latin cross leads to the conclusion that the horizontal crossbar is representative of the female. The vertical or upright portion is representative of the male. Male and female are the only two humans required to create life and perpetuate the race. That has always been sacred regardless of what people worship. Ancient Egyptian Thebans did worship a *mother/father* god.

Calvary Cross: This cross is a Latin cross mounted on a base with three steps or levels. Usually they are made of marble. There is never an image of Jesus on the Calvary cross, because it is supposed to symbolize Redemption and Ascension, not suffering. The three levels the cross is mounted on represent the Christian beliefs in Faith, Hope, and Charity. The greatest of these is Charity (Love).

Many theologians believe this cross has become too important to Christian worshipers. People use the Calvary cross as an idol, or graven image, in praying instead of having a true faith in Jesus Christ within them. It is a symbol that has taken on a meaning other than what Christianity teaches. People worship the Calvary cross instead of the teachings of Christianity that Jesus is their God and the only one to worship. It is rather ridiculous to claim there is one God only then pay homage to a cross, which is nothing more than an idol, or graven image.

Celtic Cross: This cross is a true representation of the fertility capabilities of a male and female human being. The circles in the center where the vertical and horizontal arms meet represent female genitalia or receptive power. The vertical and horizontal bars represent male genitalia, which is the reproductive power of males. Our ancient ancestors were not embarrassed by the fact that men and women must copulate to create progeny for the continuation of the human race. Christianity changed that thinking when it started to teach that children are conceived in sin. It also introduced the belief that copulation (sex) is a dirty word. Many people have a genuine problem with those teachings of the church.

Ancient records confirm that some of the early church fathers suffered from gynophobia. By studying the history of Popes it becomes apparent that following Saint Peter, the first Pope, they developed into misogynous men. It may come as a surprise to learn that St. Peter and several of the Popes to follow him were married. In Christianity the true meaning of the Celtic cross is glossed-over and we are now taught the symbols stand for heaven and earth, not male and female.

The Celtic race of people was advanced in many things. Even Caesar marveled at their knowledge. They believed in the ritual of fertility. People must produce children to perpetuate the race. Likewise, if the crops do not grow many people may starve. The Celtic cross was powerful symbolically to assure the crops would grow to provide adequate food for the people. The Celtic celebration of spring must have been a lavish affair. Eventually that celebration was included in the Christian Easter celebration when the Council of Nicaea voted the 'Easter Rule' and included the spring fertility pagan celebration into Christianity, along with Jesus voted a god and a cross symbol.

Tau Cross: The 19th letter of the Greek alphabet is Tau. The 23rd letter of the Hebrew alphabet is Tav. Both letters are pronounced the same as if they were *taw*. Many ancient people used this symbol to represent a cross. The name for the Tau cross actually comes from the Greek name. If it came from Hebrew the name would be Tav.

In Exodus 12:22-23 the Israelites are told to, *"dip a bunch of hyssop in blood and touch the lintel and doorstep. The Lord will pass over that house and not allow the destroyer to enter your house and slay you."* It is believed the shape people painted on their house in blood was a Tau cross. The Hebrew celebration of Passover originates from this so-called direction from God. They are charged to keep it forever, because, *"God passed over the houses of the people of Israel in Egypt, when he slew the Egyptians but spared the Israelites."* Many people have a real problem with the Biblical stories about a God that slays so many people and believes in war to settle differences.

In John 3:14 Jesus says, *"and as Moses lifted up the serpent in the wilderness, so must the son of man be lifted up."* That sentence leads some scholars to believe Jesus was hung on a Tau cross, which would have been similar to the rod of Moses. In Ezekiel 9: 4-6 we are told that, *"people with the mark on their forehead are to be spared, slay old men outright, young men and maidens, little children and women, but touch no one upon whom is the mark."* Why would God slay little children?

The Tau cross has an ancient history and can be traced through other world cultures. It is known that St. Francis was fond of the passage in Ezekiel when the faithful were signed on the forehead with the letter Tau. Two years before his death St. Francis received the stigmata, or wounds of Christ, in his body. The Franciscan coat of arms has crossed hands showing nail wounds and a Tau cross behind the hands. American Indians and South American tribes used the symbol. In ancient Egyptian hieroglyphics the ankh is shaped like the Tau cross, but has an oval-shaped loop on top. The oval represents female and the Tau is for male—joined together they mean *life*.

Swastika: This cross is actually a Greek or St. George cross with each of the four arms bent at a right angle to form the pattern. Current day people relate this cross to Adolph Hitler and the Nazi regime in WWII. In 1908 Guido von List of Vienna formed a secretive Armanen Society and adopted the swastika as their symbol. German mythology used the swastika as a symbol for a pure race of white skinned people that worshipped the sun. The sun worshippers in mythology were supposedly all born with an inherent superiority over all other races of people. Hitler was a latecomer to the Armanen Society; however, it did lay the groundwork for the ideals of the Aryan-Germanic beliefs that cost the lives of so many Jewish people.

It is a pity that such an ancient and ubiquitous symbol has been so maligned by the German Nazi regime. The earliest known record of the swastika cross being used was in Mesopotamia prior to 2000 B.C.E. The symbol stood for good fortune and prosperity in that society. Later the Navajos Indians in North America and the Maya in South America used the symbol.

Currently, the swastika cross is revered in both Buddhism and Hinduism. People in India use the swastika to represent a saint. The four extensions bent at a right angle are a reminder of the four places for rebirth in those religions. Those religions teach that you can be reborn as an animal or plant, a human being on earth, as a spirit, or you can be reborn in Hell. The doorways of Hindu homes have a swastika over it. When the arms are bent to the right it is a symbol of the sun, which passes from the east then appears to pass from south to west in the Northern Hemisphere. The arms bent to the left represent night and the time for all sorts of magical practices.

Kali is the goddess the swastika represents in India. Many Christian tombs in the Middle East have a swastika on the headstone. It was used as a secret symbol to represent Christ's cross during the time it was dangerous to be identified as a member of the Christian sect. Many Jewish people believe it is rather ironic that so many ancient Christian graves have a swastika when that was the symbol used by Hitler's Nazi regime in World War II to exterminate their ancestors.

During a trip to Egypt, as a guest of the government, the Minister of Mines gave orders to our guide that nothing was off-limits to my associate from Belgium or me. Our purpose was to evaluate the possibility of mining phosphate in the desert. Later, the guide suggested we might like to see an ancient necropolis that was off-limits to tourists and always had a guard present. Of course we accepted. It was a gruesome place. One small temple still had channels where blood ran during sacrifices. Most shocking, however, was the presence of swastika symbols carved in some gravestones.

Maltese Cross: This cross is also known as the Cross Pattee-Nowy. It is not used on the flag of Malta, as some people believe. The most current common use of the Maltese cross is by the Fire Service. A Fireman's badge is a somewhat compressed version of the cross that has eight distinct points. There are two points on the end of each arm.

During the 11th century the Hospitalers, or Knights of Hospitalers, as they became known due to their charitable acts, used this cross for identity. Originally the Hospitalers were known as the Knights of Saint John of Jerusalem. It was a charitable, non-military organization. Even today in the Masonic Lodge there is a Hospitalers Fund used for the purpose of charity.

The Knights of St. John moved to the Island of Malta after assisting the Crusaders to set up hospitals and hospices during the attempt to win back the Holy Land. After the order moved to Malta their cross was called the Maltese cross. The Knights Templars disappeared from France in 1307. After they left France the Papacy gave their land holdings to the Hospitalers. The vast wealth of gold, jewels, and money owned by the Knights Templars was never found. There is reason to believe their wealth may be buried on Oak Island in Newfoundland.

The Knights of St. John represented the principles of:

- Charity
- Loyalty
- Chivalry
- Gallantry
- Generosity to friend and foe
- Protection of the weak
- Dexterity in service

Their enemies resorted to throwing glass bombs filled with naphtha during the Crusades. Also, enemies sailed their vessels containing rosin, sulfur, naphtha, and flaming oil into the knights' vessels. The Knights of St. John performed many heroic deeds by rescuing their comrades from flaming vessels, and extinguishing fires.

The Fire Service chose the Maltese cross as their insignia, because it represents the ideals of saving lives and extinguishing fires. The Maltese cross is actually a variation of the Greek or St. George cross.

Star of David: ✦ The Star of David is not actually a cross, but is the nearest symbol to a cross for the Jewish people. The Jews never developed the cult of saints that blossomed in Christianity from the Jewish prophets. In Psalms it refers to the 'righteous one' who loves the law of the Lord and constantly meditates on the Lord's law. To maintain the purity in their faith many religious Jews referred to themselves as 'the pious ones.' That term developed into the Jewish name of Hasidim. Even today Jews that practice Hasidism will segregate themselves from other Jews.

In 1948 the Star of David became a symbol on the flag of the new State of Israel. It is another very ancient symbol that has represented different things throughout history. Probably the more correct name for this symbol would be to call it the Seal of Solomon. Ancient writings during the time of Solomon use this symbol, which developed later in Hebrew mythology. In 1354 Charles IV gave Jews the right to use the Star of David on a flag to represent their community in Prague, Czechoslovakia.

During the Middle Ages both Muslims and Christians used the symbol on Bibles and other artifacts in churches. The ancient Jews never had a symbolic representation for their faith. They worshipped only God and not graven images as taught in the Torah. The Star of David evolved over time as the Jewish counterpart to the Christian Latin Cross. In Nazi Germany every Jew had to wear a yellow Star of David sewn on outer clothing to confirm their heredity.

The equilateral hexagram is a six-pointed star developed by placing two equilateral triangles one on top of the other with one apex pointing up and the apex of the other triangle inverted or pointing down. There are many mystical meanings to this symbol. Perhaps the oldest symbolism is the upward pointing triangle represents a male and the one pointing down a female. In all religions there is symbolism that denotes balance such as yin/yang, male/female, good/evil, and dark/light.

The Masonic symbol is a compass with extended points placed on a square with the right angle of the square pointing down. The width of the compass points is equal to the distance between the extreme outer points of the square when the tools are properly placed. It is interesting to note that if a line is drawn to connect the compass points and another line to connect the ends of the square the resulting figure is a Star of David. Masons would call the symbol the 'Seal of Solomon.' Masonic teachings use the symbolism of building King Solomon's Temple to develop allegories that teach each participant how to conduct their life in the quest to become better men.

Mathematics – Numbers

The search for Truth ultimately leads to Mathematics, or Numbers as Plato called it. In the *Epinomis,* Plato wrote, "Numbers are the highest degree of knowledge, and that Numbers is knowledge itself." Numbers are abstract, but exceedingly important in conveying thought. Aristotle referred to using numbers as a metaphor when he wrote, "but the greatest thing of all is to be master of the metaphor; it cannot be taught by others; it is also a sign of original genius, because a good metaphor implies intuitive perception of similarity in dissimilar things." A metaphor is one thing conceived as representing another: a symbol.

Plato developed the essence of the Pythagorean doctrine. The *Epinomis, Timaeus,* and *Theaetetus* are good educational readings to study his thoughts during the dialogs about harmonics, symmetry, symphonic, astronomy, and many other things. An especially fascinating sentence is in the *Timaeus* when Plato writes, "and it was then that all these kind of things thus established received their shapes from the Ordering One, through the action of Ideas and Numbers." People think of Plato and others as ancient ancestors that were limited in knowledge. Plato thought the same thing as he refers to knowledge that came from the ancients, even though he lived nearly 500 years before Christianity.

The Pythagorean Brotherhood was established in Sicily and Calabria approximately 500BC. It was a secret organization consisting of three degrees. The third degree was the Mathematicians. They had been through the training in the Laws of Numbers and had completed all of the initiation process. Each initiate took an oath of secrecy. Aristotle was a student of Plato's and devoted his studies to rhythms and harmonics. The mathematical knowledge of equations, constants, geometry, ratios, etc were held to be sacred within the Brotherhood. Without their knowledge of Numbers the outstanding architectural achievements now enjoyed in Europe would not have been possible. The Golden Section, roots and squares of numbers and how they control shapes, construction of pentagram (star), pentagon, triangles, and many more are of utmost importance.

The secret Pythagorean Brotherhood passed along knowledge and dealt with each other by using metaphors, which only the initiated brotherhood understood the true meaning. The populace would interpret the statement literally, and did not understand the true meaning of the metaphor. That method of communication was also used in the Ancient Mysteries.

VESICA PISCIS: One very interesting verse in the Bible is John 21:11, *"So Simon Peter went aboard and hauled the net ashore, full of large fish, 153 of them; and although there were so many of them the net was not torn."* Later in verse 17 it says, *"Peter was grieved because he said to him the third time, Do you love me?"* Is there any significance between the **153** fish and the writers of John having Jesus ask the question **3** times? Many years earlier, Pythagoras had predicted in a similar situation that he could tell his followers in advance the number of fish they would catch. The Jesus story is obviously a metaphoric method of conversation to conceal the true meaning of the information being conveyed.

The number 153 is the divisor used to establish the square root of the number 3. The dividend is 265. Dividing 265 by 153 results in a quotient of 1.732, which is the square root ($\sqrt{\ }$) of 3. The square root of 3 is the controlling factor for an equilateral triangle. The number 1.732 is also the tangent of a 60° triangle. If you divide 153 by 265 the quotient is .577, which is the cotangent of 60°. An important constant is $1 \div \sqrt{3} = .577$. The beautiful cathedral in Milan, Italy was designed by using the symmetry of the square root of 3. The *Vesica Piscis* was also a constant used in the design of the arches for that cathedral. The drawings for the Milan Cathedral are the only known plans that have survived from the Renaissance Period.

Vesica in Latin means bladder. *Piscis* means fish in Latin. The *Vesica Piscis* is the area created when two circles of the exact same radius intersect when the center of one circle is drawn from any point on the circumference of the other circle.

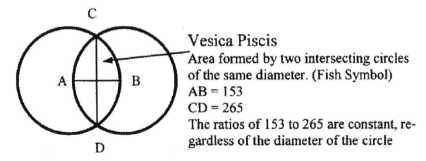

Vesica Piscis
Area formed by two intersecting circles of the same diameter. (Fish Symbol)
AB = 153
CD = 265
The ratios of 153 to 265 are constant, regardless of the diameter of the circle

Line AB is also the side of an equilateral triangle.
The other sides are formed by drawing a straight line
from A to C and B to C

The Greek word for fish is *Icthys* and was used by early Christians as a code word for Jesus. Today, you will see the 'sign of the fish' used in many places by Christians and especially on the back of automobiles. It makes one wonder why people have to advertise they are Christians? Is the fish a graven image? The mystic cult of Orphism used the name Icthys for their god-man Adonis many centuries before Christianity. The 'sign of the fish' is another case of Christianity taking beliefs and symbols from the Ancient Mysteries then claiming them to be original with Christianity. After canonization or adopting them as dogma the masses do not question the church fathers about the validity. Only those initiated could enter heaven in the ancient mysteries. Likewise, Christianity declared later that only Christians could enter heaven and still believe it to be true. The Christian idea of purgatory was also taken from Orphism. Orpheus was the legendary musician whose music had the power to move inanimate objects. He never did rescue his wife Eurydice from Hades.

The symbolic area of the intersection of two circles represents many things other than a fish. Between individuals it can be common ground, shared vision, or mutual understanding. The human eye is a vesica piscis shape. Look at the back of a one-dollar bill and you find the all Seeing Eye at the top of a pyramid. The beautiful arches in Gothic architecture were constructed using vesica piscis and the square root of three as the controlling factor. Lesser-known and embarrassing to modern day Christians is the early church's use of the vesica piscis to represent the female vulva from which life sprang forth. In many churches and paintings there are representations of Jesus in front of a vesica piscis design. Sheila-na-gig statues and carvings in churches all over the British Isles and Europe depicted a naked woman squatting with her knees apart, displaying her vulva, shown as a *vesica piscis*. Some figures present the vesica with hands pulling from each side to form a more perfect shape. Victorian prudery defaced and destroyed many of them. They came to be known as Sheelas and are thought to have originated with the Celts. [1&2]

One time in an Australian coalmine the miners were using the term sheela. After asking them what sheela meant, one bloke said, "Yank, you're ten thousand miles from home and don't even know the meaning of whore." Another time in a pub I offered to buy the pints of beer for a group of miners. One big brawny Aussie coalminer indignantly said, "Mate, I'm in the chair and it is my turn to shout." After asking him what that meant in Australian he explained, "when it is your turn to buy the beers it means you are in the chair

---

[1&2] *Woman's Dictionary of Symbols and Sacred Objects and Encyclopedia of Religion,* Macmillan

and shout means to pay." He also said it was rude to butt in and not take your turn in the chair. After apologizing for my rudeness they suggested that one present Yank should get familiar with Aussie customs. Metaphorically in Australian coal miner language if you say 'Shout for Sheela' it means 'buy a whore.' The new terms were never used, but they did contribute to my education on metaphorical language.

It is fascinating to study the anatomy of churches. Vitruvius, the master architect, wrote an architectural book in 100 B.C. that still exists. The church and papacy in Rome agreed that churches and cathedrals should be designed according to the teachings of Vitruvius. Many symbols depict most anything the mind is capable of creating and they are carved in stone and wood around the world.

Probably the most used symbols, but least known by present-day congregations, are the beautifully curved arches on the entrance to churches and cathedrals are the top half of a vesica piscis. The symbolic meaning is that the faithful must first pass through the vesica piscis (vulva), and then through the narthex, to arrive in the nave (womb) where Mother Church will comfort and protect her followers. The church's symbolism means it is a reverse passage through the birth canal to arrive where you were the most protected during your entire lifetime, namely your mother's womb. The faithful will always have a symbolic umbilical cord to Mother Church. A rose carved at the apex of many vesica piscis arches is symbolic of the only human organ designed solely for pleasure as we are taught in anatomy, which is the female clitoris. Prudery was not a problem for our ancestors.

The ancients through complicated mathematical reasoning assigned the number 2 as the female number and 3 as the male number. Five is the number for love (2 plus 3 equals 5) and 7 is the virgin number. Seven was chosen because a circle cannot be divided into seven parts by the construction of using a compass. Number 12 will be explained under Fibonacci Number Series. The suggestion is to look around the next church you enter and closely observe the artistic symbolism of using numbers. The use of symbolic numbers 2, 3, 5, 7 and 12 may surprise you.

Using your eyes to see and your brain to comprehend the symbolism will be a learning exercise. Also, there are many good books available by authors that have spent years researching the anatomy of churches. Your newfound knowledge may even help educate the preacher unless he has studied ancient architecture and numeric symbolism. In fact, studying the symbolism seems more like taking a course in pornography than anything to do with religion. Regardless of the mythical and symbolic use, the *vesica piscis* is one of the more important mathematical calculations.

GOLDEN SECTION, GOLDEN RATIO, or Golden Number is one of the most outstanding algebraic expressions. The golden ratios were used to design ancient Greek temples, European Cathedrals, and are commonly used today in designing anything that is pleasing to the eye. It is also known as the 'divine proportion.' The Greek letter Phi (**Φ)** is used to represent the Golden Section in formulas. Golden Section definition:

The ratio of the whole to the larger portion is the same as the ratio of the larger portion to the smaller portion. It is the positive root of $X^2 = X + 1$. Solving this formula results in the positive root of **1.618** golden section and a golden negative root of **-.618.** The golden section can also be defined:

$1 + \dfrac{\sqrt{5}}{2} = 1.618$ positive root, and: $\dfrac{\sqrt{5}}{2} - 1 = .618$ negative root.

If you draw a square exactly one inch on each side, then bisect the base for point (B) and use the bisect point for a center, swing an arc from (A) the upper right corner to the plane of the base to make a golden line that is 1.618 inches long (1" + .618"). By drawing a vertical, then horizontal line (dotted lines) to make a small rectangle it will form a golden rectangle that is .618" wide x 1" vertical. The larger golden rectangle is 1.618" wide x 1" vertical. The proportions of these rectangular shapes are the most pleasing to the human eye.

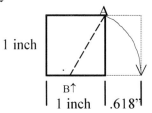

1 inch

B↑
1 inch   .618"

Note:
The length of the dashed line (hypotenuse) from B to A is the √5÷2, another important function of the Golden Section

To Solve:

$X^2 = X + 1$, subtracting $X + 1$ from both sides $= X^2 - X - 1 = 0$
Quadratic equation $= ax^2 + bx + c = 0$

Solve by: $X = -b \pm \dfrac{\sqrt{b^2 - 4ac}}{2a}$

Therefore: $X =$ unknown $\quad a = 1, \quad b = -1, \quad c = -1$

$X = \dfrac{-(-1) \pm \sqrt{(-1)^2 - 4(1)(-1)}}{2(1)} = \dfrac{1 \pm \sqrt{1+4}}{2} = \dfrac{1 \pm \sqrt{5}}{2} =$

$\dfrac{1 \pm 2.236}{2} =$ **1.618** positive root and **-.618** negative root for **X**

Phi (Φ) or 1.618 is an irrational number that cannot be expressed in terms of two integers. Like Pi (π), the ratio of the diameter of a circle to the circumference, it can be carried out thousands of places beyond the decimal point and it never stops. One college carried it out to 10 million places and found there is no repeating pattern like dividing the integers of 10 and 3 or 10÷3=3.3333333333333......etc.

The human body can literally be called a 'golden creation.' Thousands of skeletons have been studied that confirm Plato's 'Ordering One' designed humans with proportions where the Golden Section (Φ or Phi) plays a dominating role. Skin and fat distort accuracy; however, look at your middle finger. The length of the longer bone will be the same length as the total length of the two shorter bones. Your navel is the exact center of your body from which many golden section ratios and others can be calculated. It is no fluke that current day female singers and actresses go to extremes to have their navel exposed. They may not know about the golden section, but they understand harmonic symmetry is pleasing to the eye. Golden ratios are not only aesthetic, but make the human body a well functioning machine.

FIBONACCI NUMBERS: In 1202 C.E. at Pisa, Italy, Filius Bonacci (nicknamed Fibonacci) discovered that starting at number 1 each successive integer is equal to the sum of the two that precede it. Example; 1, 1, 2, 3, 5, 8, 13, 21, 34, 55, 89, 144, 233, 377....etc. The amazing thing is that these numbers trend asymptotically towards the Golden Section of 1.618 or 34÷21=1.619, 55÷34=1.618, 89÷55=1.618, 144÷89=1.618, 233÷144=1.618, 377÷233=1.618......etc.

Before getting too carried away from learning that your body is a 'Golden Creation' of ratios it should be pointed out that animal, plant, sea life, and other things were created or grow in a similar manner. Plato refers to 'dynamic symmetry' in the *Theaetetus*. Dynamic and harmonic symmetry created by the √3, √5, 1.618, -.618, and other ratios are pleasing to observe and create practical things. An athlete for example with Fibonacci numbers of a 55-inch chest and a 34-inch waist (55÷34=1.618) is a true specimen of a man, 'a hulk.' A female with a 34-inch bust and 21-inch waist (34÷21=1.619) is pleasing for both males and females to observe. Using golden section ratios created most of the old masters paintings we like so well. Buildings like the Greek Parthenon and the statues and paintings of Michelangelo, Egyptian pyramids, and many temples are true beauty as a result of balance and harmonious arrangement.

The Fibonacci number totaling 144 is the only one that is also a perfect square of another number, which is 12x12=144. The symbolic use of number 12 goes back to ancient times. The twelve disciples of Pythagoras were later referred to by New Testament writers as the 12 disciples of Jesus. The twelve tribes referred to in the Old Testament and many other items used the sacred number twelve. The sons born miraculously of virgins in mythical tales were all god/men with 12 disciples or followers. The number 12 is also the phenomenon of a sphere. Pythagoras discovered that a perfectly round ball (sphere) when touched by other spheres of exactly the same size there would be 12 spheres touching the center sphere, and touching each other. If uniform pressure is applied to the outer surface of the 12 spheres the center sphere (number13) will be compressed into a perfect dodecahedron, which is a geometric figure with 12 surfaces of equal area.

This mathematical discovery was also a major contribution to the symbolic lore associated with the number 12 as it relates to the number 13 at the center. It has even carried through to the modern day court system where there are 12 jurors (12 men in a box) and the 13th person required to be present is the judge. The 12 signs of the zodiac, 12 inches in a foot, two 12-hour periods form a day, 12 months in a year, 12 eggs in a dozen, Twelfth Night, and many others are significant examples of the number twelve. In WWII we had 12 B-24 Liberators in a squadron. The 12 bombers formed the best geometric configuration for aerial warfare. Many schoolteachers will tell you that 12 students in a class is the perfect number.

In botany, the 'Ordering One' introduced the logarithmic curve (spiral) along with the golden ratio to arrange the growth of limbs and other plant life in a pattern to receive maximum sunshine. As a higher form of life we often upset that pattern by pruning plants in the wrong place. Often times at my tree farm it is obvious that trees will do better by leaving the pruning shears in the barn. Many other items could be covered in a mathematics discussion such as the discovery by the Pythagoreans how to develop the pentagram (5-pointed star), hexagon (6-sides), etc. To be accepted into the Pythagorean Brotherhood's third degree of Mathematicians the candidate was required to create a pentagram (pentacle) on the trestle board using only the compass, square, and ruler and explain the procedure, which also created a pentagon by connecting the points of the star. Hippocrates was supposedly ejected from the Brotherhood for divulging the secret of creating the 5-pointed star by using only compass and ruler.

There are scholars that believe Pythagoras has received too much credit for the mathematics attributed to him. He did study in Egypt for a lengthy period before returning to his home country to teach. Did he gain his knowledge of mathematics in Egypt under the oath of secrecy and then return home to start a similar school using the mandatory oath of secrecy for initiates? Of course, no one knows the answer, but the similarities are remarkable between Egyptian knowledge and philosophy, Pythagorean teachings, and current day teachings in the Masonic Lodge. Mathematics taught by Pythagoras was used several thousand years earlier in Egypt to build the pyramids and temples. In a Masonic Lodge the candidate is taught that the working tools of a Master Mason (third degree) are the compass, square, and 24-inch gauge (ruler). The same tools used in the Pythagorean Brotherhood!

THEORY OF RELATIVITY: No mathematics discussion should ignore Dr. Albert Einstein. The formula he developed of $E=mc^2$ took humanity from a Newtonian world view that space and time are absolutes. The question that Isaac Newton could not answer was: How do light and gravitational force travel through the emptiness of space? The speed of light was finally determined to be 186,272 miles per second. Sound moves at 12.5 miles per second.

Dr. Einstein discovered two very important facts about light and all other electromagnetic radiation.

1. Speed never changes even if an observer is moving directly toward the light source or directly away from it. Nothing else in the universe behaves in this manner. For example, if two automobiles are traveling toward each other at 60 miles per hour the speed of the other automobile relative to each driver is 120 miles per hour. If they are traveling parallel to each other the relative speed is 0 miles per hour. With light the relative speed remains constant.

2. The speed of light at 186,272 miles per second is the speed limit of the universe. Nothing can travel faster than 186,272 miles per second.

The formula $E=mc^2$ means that energy and mass are the same things, but in different forms. Mass is frozen energy and the formula means that equivalent energy (E) is equal to the mass (m) times the speed of light squared. High School algebra tells you that by squaring the speed of light $(186,272)^2$ the result is a very large number: a number too large to comprehend. If you substitute just a few pounds for mass (m) in the equation and multiply by the speed of light squared it results in an even larger number. The larger number is pure energy (E), which is equivalent to adding just a few ounces or pounds to the formula.

A five-pound ball dropped from high altitude would penetrate most roofs. If you convert that five-pound ball to pure energy (E) by squaring the speed of light and multiply by the weight of the ball, this results in the pure energy available. From the seemingly simple formula all types of nuclear power are developed.

Nothing can exceed the speed of light, because the faster an object travels the more its mass increases. Mass approaches the infinite as the object approaches the speed of light. Since energy is required to move mass the energy would also approach the infinite. What this tells you is that to move anything faster than the speed of light it would require more energy than what is available in the entire universe.

The concept is difficult to understand because it contradicts our everyday experiences and our common sense. Space and time are not absolutes as we used to believe. The formula is quite simple. Our problem is that most of our thinking is still back in the Newtonian Age and we are currently living in an Atomic Age. Space and time are not absolutes as we believed before Dr. Einstein's ($E=mc^2$) formula was developed. The Theory of Relativity works by generating electric power daily and in testing bombs for warfare; however, the concept seems absurd to our reasoning.

INCOMPREHENSIBLE NUMBERS: The invention of computers has been a tremendous aid in handling large numbers. Unfortunately, they have been of little help in educating most of us to comprehend the large numbers required to even talk about our universe. The speed of light doubled pales in comparison when using light years to describe the distance to planets or stars. A light year is 5.88 trillion miles (5.88×10^{12})[1].

The sun is 93 million miles from the earth and the nearest star to the sun, Alpha Centauri, is 4.3 light years from earth. To calculate the miles to Alpha Centauri the 4.3 light years must be multiplied by 5.88 trillion, which is an incomprehensible number to most of us. The nearest clearly defined galaxy to earth is Andromeda, which is 2.2 million light years away.

The distance in light years to Andromeda is longer than humans have supposedly lived on earth when counting in just plain years. My brain cells have a problem with trying to comprehend just how far those distances are. Since the sun is earth's closest star at a mere hop and a jump of only ninety three million miles let's try to put that enormous distance into perspective.

Most of us older people believe that 60 miles per hour is a comfortable rate of speed when making an enjoyable trip. At 60 miles per hour you will travel 60 miles in one hour by simple arithmetic. To travel 93 million miles at 60 miles per hour would take you $93,000,000 \div 60 = 1,550,000$ hours. To find days it is $1,550,000$ hours $\div 24$ hours $= 64,583.33$ days.

---

[1] *Science and Technology Desk Reference,* Carnegie Library, Gale Research, Inc. 1993, for all references to Distance, Speed, & Light Years.

To reduce the days traveled into years it is 64,583.33 days÷365 days per year=176.94 years, which would require a steady pace of 1,440 miles driven per day. You would have no time to stop for eating, sleeping, or rest stops for nearly 177 years. Most of us can comprehend those numbers; however, it would take 100 years longer than the average life span if you could make a leisurely automobile trip to vacation on the sun.

The largest number named in the King James Bible is a thousand thousand, which is one million. (1,000,000) The Revised Standard Version changed the story to read, *"Zerah the Ethiopian came out against them with a million men and three hundred Chariots and came as far as Meresha."*[1] That is an extremely large number for Biblical writers to use. The size of the number was probably exaggerated to impress readers that Zerah's army was larger than common folks could comprehend.

One of the first people to use large astronomical numbers in a factual manner was Galileo, which caused him serious trouble with the church hierarchy in Rome. The church reaction to the science of Galileo was similar to a TV show conversation when one gang member was telling another member about a fellow in a rival gang: "man, we gotta take that baby out (kill him) cause that dude jus ain't thinkin like us good boys." The ecclesiastical boys in Rome voted to kill 'the dude' Galileo because his proven science differed with their beliefs and proved the Bible to be incorrect.

Galileo Galilei (1564–1642), a mathematician, astronomer and physicist, expanded the work of Copernicus. His pendulum calculations resulted in the Dutch developing a reliable clock. He improved the telescope and made major astronomy discoveries like explaining sunspots, discovered the moons of Jupiter, and proved the sun and earth rotate on an axis. On June 21, 1633, Galileo was found guilty by the Roman Catholic Church for proving the earth revolves around the sun and is not the center of the universe. His calculations completely destroyed the church teachings from the Bible that the universe consists of three levels, which were thought to be Heaven, Earth, and Hell. God lived in heaven, humans lived on earth, and Satan ruled Hell, the place below.

To reduce his sentence, Galileo, who was a friend of the Pope, signed a document disavowing what he had proven and agreed to never teach such blasphemy as long as he lived. The church restricted him to his home near Florence, Italy for the rest of his life. The almost unbelievable result of the story is that the Vatican on December 28, 1991, officially admitted that the mathematician Galileo Galilei was correct and the Catholic Church, as well as

---

[1] 2 Chronicles 14:9 RSV

the Bible, had been wrong about the shape of the universe and the place of human beings and earth within the universe. It took 328 years of pressure from the scientific community and others to have the Vatican renounce the sentence and finally admit the church and Bible were wrong.

Our discussion about mathematics and incomprehensible large numbers reminds me of an Appalachian mountain boy that couldn't pass the physical exam in WWII. He wanted to contribute to the war effort and walked to town for a free course offered in machine shop practice. After his first lesson on the micrometer he was impressed and excitedly told his mother about those itty-bitty things called thousandths of an inch. Mama asked her boy just how many of those things there were in an inch. He answered his mother by saying, "oh my God mama, they are so tiny that an inch must have millions of them things."

If there is a moral to the Appalachian story, or an explanation of astronomically large numbers it might be; for us non-mathematicians large numbers are only what each individual perceives them to be in their mind.

One other practical branch of mathematics is trigonometry, which deals with the relationships between the sides and angles of triangles. Boy Scouts are always amazed to learn how easy it is to calculate the distance to points they cannot reach when hiking. Some practical calculations can be made with nothing more than a six-inch ruler and the simple digits of 3, 4, and 5 as shown below. If you connect any three items (say sticks, straws, or strings) with the exact lengths of 3 inches, 4 inches, and 5 inches, or any multiple of those numbers, a perfect 90-degree angle will be formed where the 3 inch and 4 inch items meet.

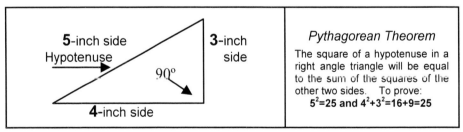

Builders often use this method to assure the foundations of buildings are perfectly square, or at right angles to each other.

We should be forever grateful to our ancient ancestors for leaving a mathematics legacy they developed through curiosity, vision, determination, and just plain old hard work with the compass, pen, and ruler. Ancient work done in conical geometry is even difficult to duplicate on today's computers.

Freemasonry

DEATH! -- Would have been the Church's (all Christianity) verdict if the following pages had been written during the Dark Ages, various Inquisitions, or the Medieval Age. To even speak any words other than the hard-line of the Church would have resulted in the same verdict. The Church was the self-appointed guardians and definers of all sacred and secular matters. Only the church had the right to decide what was Truth, what scriptural works were of God, and which were spurious. Works that supported the Pauline theology were approved canon. All others that told the Truth in any other way were declared heretical including all oral tradition.

The vast knowledge of ancient civilizations was of no importance. The Roman church suppressed every rival. Previous beliefs that brought initiates into intimate contact with the divine reality of God were classed heretical, absolutely forbidden, and punishable by death. To maintain the wisdom and knowledge of ancient societies there was no choice but to go underground. Hidden wisdom had to be passed secretly from master to pupil otherwise it would be lost. Cathedrals were built that people believed were for Christianity when in reality they exemplified the hidden streams of spirituality so detested by the Church.

[1]Chartres Cathedral in France is the epitome of suppressed spiritual truths that were exemplified in stone so that non-initiates could not detect the message. There is not one single depiction of the crucifixion that dates from the twelfth century in the cathedral. Rosslyn Chapel in Scotland is the culmination of hidden wisdom and truths carved into stone for only the enlightened to understand. Rosslyn Chapel is probably the most unusual and least understood building that exists today. Every item and stone carving in the building depicts beliefs or truths that go back to the ancient roots of Freemasonry, which pre-dates Christianity by several thousand years.

Many people cannot comprehend how men from Christian, Judaism, Buddhist, Muslim, Taoist, Confucian, and other religions that believe in a Supreme Being can participate in Freemasonry together and not have conflicts or differences. *"Freemasonry is not a religion and lacks the basic elements of religion. It has no dogma or theology, no wish or means to enforce religious orthodoxy. It offers no sacraments. It does not claim to lead to salvation by works, by secret knowledge, or by any other means. Discussion of religion, politics, or any controversial subject within a duly constituted Masonic Lodge is strictly prohibited."* (See page 84, paragraph 2)

---

[1] *ROSSLYN, Guardian of the Secrets of the HOLY GRAIL*, Murphy & Hopkins, Element Books, Ltd. 2000

The Fraternity of Free and Accepted Masons is the oldest, largest, and most widely known fraternal organization in the world. Some historians trace Freemasonry to the Tenth Century, B.C. during the building of King Solomon's Temple. Records reveal that Freemasonry was introduced into England in 926 A.D. There are approximately 4,000,000 Freemasons in the United States, which is two-thirds of the worldwide membership.

The basic unit in Freemasonry is the Symbolic Lodge, which is commonly known as the "Blue Lodge." In the Jurisdiction of Pennsylvania there are more than 600 Blue Lodges with membership of approximately 250,000. The Blue Lodge confers three Symbolic Degrees known as:

1. Entered Apprentice
2. Fellow Craft
3. Master Mason

Membership is limited to adult males who can meet the recognized qualifications and standards of character and reputation. A man becomes a Freemason through his own volition. No one is asked to join its ranks. When a man seeks admission to a Symbolic Lodge (Blue Lodge) it is of his own free will and accord. The choice is entirely his. One of the customs of Freemasonry is not to solicit members. One seeking admission must have a desire and must request a petition form from one whom he believes to be a Mason.

The petitioner must be recommended by two members of a Masonic Lodge and pass a unanimous ballot. The petitioner must be 21 years of age, mentally and physically competent, of good moral character, and believe in the existence of a Supreme Being.

Freemasonry is not a secret society. It does not hide its existence or its membership. There has been no attempt to conceal the purpose, aims, and principles of Freemasonry. It is an organization formed and existing on the broad basis of Brotherly Love, Relief (Charity), and Truth. Its constitutions are published for the world to behold. Its rules and regulations are open for inspection.

It is true that Freemasonry has modes of recognition, rites, and ceremonies with which the world is not acquainted. In this regard, all human groups and institutions have private affairs. For instance, families have discussions on subjects which do not, and should not, concern their neighbors.

Freemasonry does not pretend to take the place of religion nor serve as a substitute for the religious beliefs of its members. Freemasonry accepts men found to be worthy, regardless of religious convictions. An essential requirement is a belief in the existence of a Supreme Being.

The charity and services rendered by Freemasonry are beyond measure, although it is not a beneficial or insurance society, and is not organized for profit. Over $2,000,000 is spent each day in Masonic Hospitals to care for sick children. Masonic Burn Centers are the world's finest medical institutions and have no billing departments. Masonic Learning Centers are tuition free for any dyslexic child. Schizophrenic treatment is free.

Freemasonry teaches monotheism. It teaches the Golden Rule. It seeks to make good men better through the firm belief in the Fatherhood of God, the Brotherhood of Man, and the Immortality of the Soul. The Tenets of Freemasonry are ethical principles that are acceptable to all good men. It teaches tolerance toward all mankind. Freemasonry proudly proclaims that it consists of men bound together by bonds of Brotherly love and affection. It dictates to no man as to his beliefs, either religious or secular. It seeks no advantage for its members through business or politics. Freemasonry is not a forum for discussion on partisan affairs.[1]

The basic and fundamental principles of Masonry are found in what is ordinarily known as "Blue Lodge Masonry." Blue Lodge Masonry consists of the first three degrees, which many men never go beyond. After receiving the third degree a man is known as a Master Mason.

The teachings in Masonry are a succession of allegories with each lesson building upon the previous lessons. The actors in the allegories practice continuously and do a very professional job. The stage settings and costumes are spectacular in the Lodge of Perfection consisting of the 4° through the 14°; the Council of Princes of Jerusalem 15°and 16°; Chapter of Rose Croix 17° and 18°; and the Consistory 19° through 32° in what is known as The Ancient and Accepted Scottish Rite. The 33° is an honorary degree. (See page 83)

Following are the names of all 33 degrees in The Ancient Accepted Scottish Rite of Freemasonry. Lessons taught in each degree are given so that you will understand the Roman Catholic Church slowly tortured and executed people if church officials believed they possessed knowledge or wisdom of that type. While reading the lessons taught in each degree ask yourself the question, *would you execute or slowly burn anyone at the stake that is found guilty of having that knowledge?* Now you should understand why Freemasonry did not reveal its existence for many years. Death and loss of irreplaceable human knowledge would result from the Church enforcing its self-appointed rights as guardian and definer of all sacred and secular matters. We can be thankful that civil laws forced Christianity to modify its position.

---

[1] Information on Pages.75-77 published by Grand Lodge of Pennsylvania 100M.7-80

Following are the names of all thirty-three degrees in the Ancient Accepted Scottish Rite of Freemasonry. After the Third Degree of Master Mason it is a lifelong learning experience that is the responsibility of each Master Mason to pursue on his own initiative.

[1]**1°-Entered Apprentice:** Apprentice means learner. This degree teaches the candidate all about the basics of the Lodge Room and how he is a part of the surroundings. A Proficiency Program is given to the candidate.

2°-Fellowcraft: At the end of an apprenticeship the candidate is examined and tested for his proficiency. If he passes then he is made a full member of the craft and called a "fellow of the craft." The degree teaches the necessity of *education* and seven Liberal Arts of: *Grammar, Rhetoric, Logic, Arithmetic, Music, Astronomy, and Geometry.* Fellow Craft represents manhood in its most splendid conception and its greatest responsibility. He understands the immensity of the tasks before him and approaches them with the joy of one who is competent and resolved to conquer. His family depends upon him for support. The Fellow Craft is strong in body, soul, spirit, and competent to cope with all of life's realities.

3°-Master Mason: This degree teaches all the rights and privileges of a Master Mason. He is taught there is no degree anywhere higher than the Third Degree, or Master Mason. There are 29 additional degrees in Scottish Rite Masonry, which will contribute to his knowledge on the subject of Masonry. Let nothing make you swerve from your duty, violate your vows to God, or betray your trust; but be true and faithful, and imitate other Masons who have always lived by the Golden rule. By example, demonstrate the precepts of Freemasonry in your daily living. To go through the Third Degree in Masonry means to die ritually and be reborn.

4°-Secret Master: This degree teaches that you have taken the first step toward the inner sanctuary and heart of the temple. You are in the path that leads up the slope to the mountain of Truth, which depends upon your secrecy, obedience, and fidelity whether you will advance or remain stationary.

5°-Perfect Master: Industry and honesty are the virtues peculiarly inculcated in this degree.

6°-Intimate Secretary: Teaches to be zealous and faithful; to be disinterested and benevolent; and to act as peacemaker in case of dissensions, disputes, and quarrels among the brethren.

---

[1] **NOTE**: The lesson taught in each degree is language from the 16th Century, which is included in the *Master Mason Bible* and may differ from current day standards of grammar, punctuation and capitalization.

7°-Provost and Judge: The lesson taught is that this Degree inculcates JUSTICE, in decision and judgment, and in our intercourse and dealing with other men.

8°-Intendent of the Building: Teaches the important lesson that none are entitled to advance in the Ancient and Accepted Scottish Rite, who have not by study and application made themselves familiar with Masonic learning and jurisprudence. Individual learning and responsibility is stressed.

9°-Master Elect of the Nine: Consecrated to bravery, devotedness, and patriotism. Protect the oppressed against the oppressor and devote yourself to the honor and interest of your country.

10°-Master Elect of the Fifteen: Devoted to same objects as 9° and also to the cause of Toleration and Liberality against Fanaticism and Persecution, political and religious. Enlightenment against Error, Barbarism, and Ignorance.

11°-Sublime Master Elected: You are to be true to all men. You must be frank and sincere in all things. Be earnest in doing whatever it is your duty to do. No man must repent that he has relied upon your resolve, your profession, or your work.

12°-Grand Master Architect: The lessons taught by the Grand Master Architect of the Universe demand much of us to perform faithfully and fully. Reflect upon the dignity of human nature, and the vast powers and capacities of the human soul. Let us begin to rise from earth toward the stars.

13°-Master of the Ninth Arch: You must find out for yourself if the legend and history of this Degree are true, or but an allegory, containing within itself a deeper truth and a more profound meaning. The Hebrews are forbidden to pronounce the Sacred Name; instead whenever it occurs they have for ages read the word *Adonai* instead.

14°-Grand Elect Mason: It is for each individual Mason to discover the secret of Masonry, by reflection upon its symbols and a wise consideration and analysis of what is said and done in the work. Masonry does not inculcate her truths. She states them once and briefly; or hints them; or interposes a cloud between them and eyes that would be dazzled by them. The practical object of Masonry is the physical and moral amelioration and the intellectual and spiritual improvement of individuals and society. Neither can be effected except by the dissemination of Truth.

15°-Knight of the East or Sword: The leading lesson of this Degree is Fidelity to obligation, and Constancy, and Perseverance under difficulties and discouragement. Masonry is engaged in a crusade against ignorance, intolerance, fanaticism, superstition, uncharitableness, and error.

16°-Prince of Jerusalem: The whole world is God's Temple. No one expects to rebuild the Temple of Jerusalem. To establish all over the world the New Law and Reign of Love, Peace, Charity, and Toleration is to build the Temple that is most acceptable to God. God's House can be under the over-arching trees, in the open, level meadows, on a hillside, in a glen, or in a city's swarming streets. Masonry is engaged in building God's Temple!

17°-Knight of the East and West: This is the first of the philosophical degrees; and the beginning of a course of instruction, which will fully unveil to you the heart of the inner mysteries of Masonry. In all time, truth has been hidden under symbols and often under a succession of allegories; where veil after veil had to be penetrated before the true light was reached and the essential truth stood revealed. Light is but the imperfect reflection of a ray of the Infinite and Divine.

18°-Knight of the Rose Croix: Each of us makes such application to his own faith and creed, of the symbols, and ceremonies of this Degree as seems to him proper. You may be reminded of ancient ceremonies in this Degree. The ceremonies of this Degree receive many different explanations; each interpreting them for himself, and not offended at the interpretation of others.

19°-Grand Pontiff: The true Mason labors for the benefit of those who are to come after him, and for the advancement and improvement of his race. All men who deserve to live, desire to survive their funerals, and to live afterward in the good that they have done mankind, rather than in the fading character written in men's memories. Most men desire to leave some work behind them that may outlast their own day and brief generation. That is an instinctive impulse, given by God, and often found in the rudest human heart; the surest proof of the soul's immortality, and the fundamental difference between man and the wisest brutes. To plant the trees that, after we are dead, shall shelter our children, is as natural as to love the shade of those our fathers planted. The rudest unlettered man, painfully conscious of his own inferiority, will toil to educate children, that they may take a higher station in the world than him; – and such are the world's greatest benefactors.

20°-Master ad Vitam: The true Mason is a practical Philosopher, who under religious emblems, in all ages adopted by wisdom, builds upon plans traced by nature and reason the moral edifice of knowledge.

21°-Patriarch Noachite: This Degree neither charges you to be modest nor humble, nor vainglorious, nor filled with self-conceit. Be not wiser in your own opinion than the Deity, nor find fault with His works, nor endeavor to improve upon what He has done. Be modest also in your intercourse with your fellows, and slow to entertain evil thoughts of them, and reluctant to ascribe to them evil intentions. Thousands of presses flood the country with information that malign the motives and conduct of men and parties, and in making one man think worse of another; while, scarcely one is found that ever, even accidentally, labors to make man think better of others. Slander was never so insolently licentious as it is today.

22°-Knight of the Royal Axe: Sympathy with the great laboring classes, respect for labor itself, and resolution to do some good *work* in our day and generation. These are the lessons of this Degree, and they are purely Masonic. Masonry is *work*. It venerates the Grand Architect of the Universe. It commemorates the building of a Temple. Its principle emblems are the working tools of Masons and Artisans. It preserves the name of the first worker in brass and iron as one of its passwords. When the Brethren meet together they are *at labor*. Genuine work alone, done faithfully, is eternal, even as the Almighty Founder and World-Builder Himself.

23°-Chief of the Tabernacle: This Degree teaches that the world is a common temple. It dramatizes how the Mysteries spread to many countries from Egypt before arriving in Greece. Even the Druids in the British Isles celebrated Dionysus, which was learned from the Egyptians. *The Mysteries of Eleusis celebrated at Athens in honor of Ceres, swallowed up, as it were all of the others taking them from barbaric nations to the holy and august Eleusinian Mysteries,* so said Cicero. Soon people in remotest lands were initiated into the Mysteries by ceremonies called initiation. The object lesson is that holy and august works will ultimately prevail.

24°-Prince of the Tabernacle: Symbols were the universal language of ancient theology. They were the most obvious method of instruction; for, like nature herself, they addressed understanding through the eye. The most ancient expressions denoting communication of religious knowledge, signify ocular exhibition. Ancient sages, both barbarian and Greek, involved their meaning in lessons that were conveyed in either visible symbols, or in those parables and sayings of old, which the Israelites consider a sacred duty to hand down unchanged to successive generations.

25°-Knight of the Brazen Serpent: This Degree is both philosophical and moral. It teaches the necessity of reformation as well as repentance as a means of obtaining mercy and forgiveness. It is also devoted to an explanation of the symbols of Masonry. Initiates were taught in the ancient Mysteries that the rule of Evil and Darkness is temporary, but that Light and Good will be eternal.

26°-Prince of Mercy: This Degree teaches that Masons value the importance of any Truth. We utter no word that can be deemed irreverent by one of any faith. We do not tell any religious organization what they should believe. To do so is beyond our jurisdiction. Masonry, of no one age, belongs to all time; of no one religion, it finds its great Truths in all. To every Mason, Wisdom or Intelligence, Force or Strength, Harmony or Fitness, and Beauty are attributes of God.

27°-Commander of the Temple: This is the first of the Chivalric Degrees. It is placed between the 26th and the last of the Philosophical Degrees to remind you that while engaged in the speculation and abstractness of philosophy and creed, the Mason is also to continue to be engaged in the active duties of this great warfare of life. He is not only a Moralist and Philosopher but also a Soldier, the successor of those Knights of the Middle Age, who, while they wore a Cross, also wielded the Sword and were the soldiers of Honor, Loyalty, and Duty. Times change, and circumstances, but Virtue and Duty remain the same. The evils to be warred against but take another shape, and are developed in a different form.

28°-Knight of the Sun: The Degree teaches that God is the author of everything that exists; the Eternal, the Supreme, the Living, and Awful Being; from whom nothing in the universe is hidden. Light and Darkness are the World's Eternal ways. God is the principal of everything that exists, and the Father of all beings. He is the Infinite Mind and Supreme Intelligence.

29°-Knight of St. Andrew: A miraculous tradition hallows the Ancient Cross of St. Andrew. This cross appeared to Achaius, King of the Scots, and Hungus, King of the Picts, the night before the battle was fought between them and Athelstane, King of England, as they were on their knees in prayer. Every cross of Knighthood is a symbol of the qualities of the Knight of St. Andrew of Scotland, which are Humility, Patience, and Self-denial.

30°-Grand Elect Knight Kadosh: The Degree teaches that we often profit more by our enemies than by our friends. *We support ourselves only on that which resists, and owe our success to opposition.* Clement the Fifth with the Pope's approval double-crossed the Knights Templars and had the Grand Master, Jacques de Molay, publicly burned in Paris on March 11, 1314 A.D. None of the Templars' vast treasures were ever recovered by Clement the Fifth of France, which was his motive in denouncing the Knights Templars on Friday the 13th October 31, 1307. Templars' ships, bearing the Skull and Crossbones Flags and filled with treasures, mysteriously sailed from the shores of France the previous night, but their work for humanity has never ceased. (NOTE: Kadosh means Holy in Hebrew.)

31°-Grand Inspector Inquisitor Commander: To hear patiently, to weigh deliberately and dispassionately, and to decide impartially are the chief duties of a Judge as this Degree teaches. The Holy Bible will remind you of your obligation; and as you judge here below, so you will be yourself judged hereafter, by One who does not submit, like an earthly judge, to the sad necessity of inferring the motives, intentions, and purposes of men from the uncertain and often unsafe testimony of their acts and words. Every soul that now is, or ever was, or ever will be on earth is and ever will be through the whole infinite duration of eternity, present and visible.

32°-Sublime Prince of the Royal Secret: We are taught in this Degree that the Occult Science of the Ancient Magi was concealed under the shadows of the Ancient Mysteries. It was imperfectly revealed or rather disfigured by the Gnostics. It is guessed at under the obscurities that cover the pretended crimes of the Templars, and it is found enveloped in the enigmas that seem impenetrable, in the Rites of the Highest Masonry. Legends and symbols still and ever conceal from the Profane, and ever preserves to the Elect the same Truths.

33°-Sovereign Grand Inspector General: This is the last Degree in the Ancient and Accepted Scottish Rite of Freemasonry. It is a rank and decoration in recognition of services to the RITE. No Mason can petition for the 33rd Degree and it is always a conferred Degree. Less that 1% of Master Masons achieve the rank of Thirty-Third Degree.[1]

The origin of the word Mason is from the Medieval Latin word 'Maconner' and means *"to build."* Maconetins means *"a builder."* All of the symbolism, pageantry, allegories, and references to the building of King Solomon's Temple are for the purpose of a Master Mason to slowly, but deliberately, build a spiritual temple within himself. No person can steal anything from that temple unless he personally approves. Only the Mason is king of his spiritual temple, which is known only to his God and the Master Mason. The Master Mason also conducts his life under a sworn obligation to always attempt, along with his brethren, to build God's Temple here on this earth for as long as there is any life left in his body.

In the preface of, *A HISTORY OF THE SUPREME COUNCIL, 33°,* For the Northern Masonic Jurisdiction, U.S.A. it states, *"Masonry is one of the most conservative of all human institutions. This is inherent in the very foundation stones on which it is built, ---the three cardinal virtues, Brotherly Love, Relief (or Charity), and Truth; and the four tenets of our profession, -- Temperance, Fortitude, Prudence, and Justice. In theory, these foundation stones are immutable, and unchangeable, but in practice, who can completely define any one of them,* **"What is Truth?"** *Also, Today most Masons are concerned with form, and very few with substance. For every hundred Masons concerned with the conferral of degrees, perhaps five or ten think of*

---

[1] See footnote on page 78 about Degree reference from the *Master Mason Bible.*

the underlying philosophy. The history of Masonry, and its philosophy for living, must still be written and explained to each generation of Masons."

Page 173 states, *"The Masonic doctrine of Universality, means, any race, creed or color, provided the individual believes in one God. White, yellow, brown, red, black; Christian, Jew, Hindu, Buddhist, Moslem, Confucian, Taoist, Zoroastrian; all are eligible for membership in the Masonic Fraternity."*

Masonic ideals played a major role in American Independence. Fifty-three Master Masons of the fifty-six men that signed The Declaration of Independence were willing to give their life to form a government based on the Universality Doctrine, three Cardinal Virtues, and four Tenets of Masonry. Those ideals could not be achieved if the Catholic or Protestant church played any role, whatsoever, in forming the new government. John Witherspoon, a former Scot Presbyterian clergyman turned educator, was the only signer with any direct affiliation to a church. He argued for the French and was critical of John Adams, calling him "stiff and tenacious of temper."

Lectures and sermons designed to have audiences believe that America was founded upon the Christian religion are misleading. Speakers should research government documents. Records will verify that the founders of America did not trust any organized religious institution.

•Thomas Jefferson, *"Millions of innocent men, women, and children, since the introduction of Christianity, have been burnt, tortured, fined, imprisoned; yet we have not advanced one inch towards uniformity. What has been the effect of the coercion? To make one half of the world fools, and the other half hypocrites. To support error and roguery all over the earth."[1]*

•James Madison pointing to Catholic and Protestant history wrote, *"Whenever 'ecclesiastical establishments' had shaped civil society, they had supported political tyranny; never had they protected the people's liberties."[2]*

•On September 18, 1793, at 10:00 AM, Masons headed by George Washington marched from Alexandria, VA to Washington, DC for the Masonic ceremony of laying the cornerstone for the US Capital. In a bronze panel, one Capital door shows Washington and others in full Masonic regalia.

•During George Washington's administration the U. S. Senate ratified a declaration that few people know about or appreciate the significance for a free society functioning under civil laws, *"The government of the United States is not, in any sense, founded on the Christian religion."[3]*

---

[1] *The Arrogance of Faith*, F G. Wood, Alfred A. Knopf, 1990

[2,3] *Treaties and International Acts of the United States Of America*, U.S Government Printing Office 1931

On June 11, 1776, the Continental Congress appointed a five-man committee of Chairman Thomas Jefferson, Benjamin Franklin, John Adams, Roger Sherman, and Robert Livingston to draft the Declaration of Independence. George Washington, Benjamin Franklin, and other founding fathers were vitally interested in the substance (philosophy) of Masonry. The many Inquisitions, Theocracy of England, witch-hunts by the Protestant church, and centuries of religious atrocities had a major influence on forming the new government. Democratic principles were established in the United States of America in spite of Catholic or Protestant Christianity. Orthodox Christians repeatedly opposed religious freedom.

A French Master Mason, Pierre Charles L'Enfant, was the architect for the basic city plan of Washington, D.C., which was laid out and built along Masonic principles.[1] Marquis de Lafayette was a French Master Mason, soldier, and politician that served on George Washington's staff. His wife embroidered a Masonic Apron for Washington that is displayed at Philadelphia in the Grand Lodge of Pennsylvania. Benjamin Franklin got major financial assistance for the Colonies from his Masonic brothers in France. Masons conducted the Boston Tea Party from St. Andrew Lodge.

Masonry is concerned only with the results of its ideals, and never advertises. Therefore, history books do not record, as such, the major Masonic influence that prevailed and guided the thinking and action of our forefathers in forming a government for the United States. Nor do history books record the underlying stability due to the Masonic philosophy during the Inquisitions when the Church was running totally out of control, torturing, killing, roasting them alive, and burning people while reporting only to itself. Church scribes even kept records of what the victim said while misogynist bishops enjoyed themselves torturing women's breasts and genitals. The result was a death so horrible that one cannot even imagine the suffering.

British authors, Michael Baigent and Richard Leigh in their book, *The Temple and the Lodge*, do a credible job tracing Masonic history. They tell the story of the 14th Century Knights Templars to the period of the Scottish King Robert the Bruce. Part four of the book covers the First American Freemasons, the War for Independence, and concludes with the Republic, which is America. Forty-nine Masonic Lodges were active in the British Army during the War of Independence, and many functioned in the Colonial troops.

The book tells the story well of how Masons from both sides visualized that America could be the embodiment of the long-standing

---

[1] *The Secret Architecture of Our Nation's Capital*, (Masonic Influence) D. Ovason, Century Books, 1999

Masonic dream for so many years: *To form a country that has freedom of religion, freedom of speech, checks and balances in the Federal Government, recognize that all people should be treated equally, help for the downtrodden, the widow, the orphan, and many other attributes of the Masonic Philosophy.*

All Americans should be indebted to the founders of our country, and especially for their Masonic ideals. The Constitution of the United States is a unique document in the history of the world. The Constitution incorporates what Freemasonry represented when it could not be revealed during the many centuries of Catholic and Protestant atrocities. In a very real sense, The Constitution of the United States is a Freemasonic document.

Many people ask, when is a man a Mason? That question is virtually impossible to answer. One very good attempt to answer the question is posted on the website of the Grand Lodge of Pennsylvania. It is question 99, and refers to one of the most popular Masonic books ever written, *The Builders*, by Joseph F. Newton. Brother Newton writes:

"When he can look out over the rivers, the hills and the far horizon with a profound sense of his own littleness in the vast scheme of things, and yet have faith, hope and courage, which is the root of every virtue. When he knows that down in his heart every man is as noble, as vile, as divine, as diabolic and as lonely as himself, and seeks to know, to forgive and to love his fellow man.

When he knows how to sympathize with men in their sorrows, yea even in their sins – knowing each man fights a hard fight against many odds. When he has learned how to make friends and to keep them and above all, how to keep friends with himself. When he loves flowers, can hunt birds without a gun and feels the thrill of an old forgotten joy when he hears the laugh of a little child.

When he can be happy and high-minded amid the meaner drudgeries of life. When star crowned trees and the glint of sunlight on flowing waters subdue him like the thought of one much loved and long dead. When no voice of distress reaches his ears in vain, and no hand seeks his aid without a response. When he finds good in every faith that helps any man to lay hold of divine things and see majestic meanings of life, whatever the faith may be. When he can look into a wayside puddle and sees something beyond mud, and into the face of the most forlorn fellow mortal and see something beyond sin.

When he knows how to pray, how to love, how to hope. When he has kept faith with himself, with his God; in his hand a sword for evil, in his heart a bit of a song; glad to live, but not afraid to die!

Such a man has found the only secret of Freemasonry, and the one, which it is trying to give the world."

- A little girl with awful burns was being admitted to the Cincinnati Masonic Burn Center operated by the Shrine. One worried director said the budget was not sufficient to cover all of her expenses. We must not think that way, said another director; *our budget must be whatever is required to restore the little girl to health!* All directors agreed.[1]

- Neighbors of a poor Pittsburgh family could not understand why a very sick boy was picked up early one Sunday morning by men they knew to be company executives, driven to a private jet, then flown to a specialty hospital for a life-saving emergency treatment. (The men were all Masons)

- On September 26, 2000, a beautiful blonde eleven-year old girl stood before an audience of over 600 men at the Pittsburgh Convention Center and gave an eloquent speech. She thanked them for giving her the opportunity to learn how to read, write, speak in public, and that she was not taken out of school for a learning disability, as recommended to her parents at age seven by public school administrators. The girl was from Ohio. Her parents had faithfully driven several days a week to Pittsburgh so she could attend the Masonic Learning Center for dyslexic children. The little girl was given an honorarium of $500.00. Later in the program she asked to return to the podium, which she did, and returned the money. The little girl requested that her $500.00 be invested in the Masonic Learning Center to help other dyslexic children. There wasn't a dry eye in the audience at the Pittsburgh Convention Center.

Thousands of situations similar to the above three could be given. The public in general would never understand why such action would ever be taken, and they will never be told. Children and parents that have been the recipients of medical help, financial aid, and educational assistance may not know the reason why such goodness takes place, but they do understand it is the philosophy of Freemasonry in action.

John. J. Robinson, a medieval historian, business executive, ex-marine, and a non-Mason was a very staunch supporter of Freemasonry and

---

[1] A *Pilgrim's Path*, Robinson, John J., page 177, M. Evans & Co., Inc. 1993.

the ideals it represents. Masonic officials in Ohio made Mr. Robinson a Mason at sight (shortened version) shortly before his death. In his book, *A Pilgrim's Path,* Freemasonry is strongly defended against attacks from the Christian Right by people such as Pat Robertson and others.

Robinson makes a plea in the book for Freemasonry to publicly defend itself against such attacks. That will never be done, because debating critics publicly is in total opposition to fundamental Masonic beliefs. It would be a waste of valuable time that should be used to pursue Masonic ideals. Masonry teaches that action taken by members of the Craft will exemplify what is truly in their hearts, which does not require any publicity.

Following are excerpts from another book, *Born in Blood,* by John J. Robinson, M. Evans & Co. 1989.

- Page 214: The G within the Masonic Compass and Square stands for Geometry. The Fellowcraft Degree teaches it is with this science that man comprehends the universe, the movement of planets, and the cycle of seasons. It is the basis for the Masonic designation of the Supreme Being as the Grand Architect of the Universe from the Masonic science of architecture.
- Page 267: Freemasonry can safely be asserted to *not* be a religion, on a simple basis. Religious creeds generally are believed by their adherents to be completely *right.* That means that they believe that all other creeds are, at least to some extent wrong. Masonry's position is the opposite; it acknowledges that there is some Truth in all men's perception of God and declines to assert that any one belief is perfect.
- In the 16th century the Earl of Shaftsbury, Anthony A. Cooper, said, "Men of sense are really of but one religion." A woman asked him, "Pray, my Lord, what religion is that which men of sense agree in?" "Madam," replied the Earl, "Men of sense never tell it." The Earl was a Master Mason.

Freemasonry is a way of life!
'Goodness freely given for its own sake'

The Greatest Story Ever Told
<u>(A one-page story)</u>

God, in ancient times, chose a virgin to give birth to His son. The virgin was informed that when the boy grew into manhood he would be a Redeemer for all of mankind. Those who believe in him and follow him will be saved from their sins. On December 25, the blessed day of the child's birth, Magi arrived bringing gifts in recognition of the new savior for mankind. All the earth rejoiced that God had created this infant boy in His likeness to be a physical representation of God among all nations.

When the godchild grew into a young man people started to gather in groups to hear His teachings, which were new to them. God's son taught them to love each other. He taught the multitudes to have respect for one another, and never take any action against another person unless you approve of similar action being done to yourself.

The godman taught people how they could be cleansed of their sins and be born again, as new people, by the use of water in a ceremony called Baptism. Admitting their wrongdoings and submitting to the cleansing power of holy water placed on their skin during the ceremony would miraculously wash their sins away. He also turned water into wine, raised people from the dead, and cured lepers.

He taught that people could be transformed into a likeness of Him by participating in a ceremony called Communion. The Savior King taught His followers how to achieve redemption by participating in a communal meal of bread and wine. Bread was symbolic of His body. Wine was symbolic of His blood. Each participant was given a wafer to eat during the ceremony with the sign of the cross on it. The words spoken were so profound that they were inscribed as: *He who will not eat of my body and drink of my blood, so that he will be made one with me and I with him, the same shall not know salvation.*

Some factions believed the Godman's teachings were blasphemy and contrived to have Him killed. He was hung on a cross or a tree. While being ridiculed someone speared him. He died on a Friday with the spear wound in His side. He was buried in a tomb with a huge boulder placed in front of the entrance. After three days, He arose on Easter Sunday from the dead and left the tomb, with the boulder rolled aside, and miraculously ascended into Heaven to be with God almighty. An anonymous poet at that time wrote:

Have they sacrificed thee? Do they say that thou hast died for them? He is not dead! He lives forever! He is alive more than they, for he is the mystic one of sacrifice. He is their Lord, living and young forever!

He died for the Salvation of mankind!

Christians reading *The Greatest Story Ever Told* may believe it is a brief description of the life of Jesus. It is not! All events in the story were ancient and well-known myths by the time stories attributed to Paul were written about his Godman Jesus, a Greek name derived from Joshua of the Jews. Christian beliefs and theology about the life of Jesus are an exact parallel to an amalgam of 'ancient mystery' stories. Biblical and historical scholars have found nothing new or different in Paul's writings than what had already been included in the ancient mysteries. Many decades after the era of Paul, theologians chose the name Christian and then claimed the writings to be literalism and unique to Christianity, rather than symbolism used in allegories. Teachings to seek 'Christ within' evolved into the word Christian.

Christian believers that have not done in-depth research, and have accepted Biblical writings and preacher's sermons as literal facts, will be chagrined to learn the story predates Christianity by many centuries. *The Greatest Story Ever Told* is primarily about the mythical god Mithra of Persia that predates Christianity by at least 600 years. Mithra had 12 disciples, was called "a Good Shepherd," and was considered "the Way, Truth and Light, the Redeemer, the Savior, and the Messiah." His sacred day was Sunday, "the Lord's Day." He was considered a great traveling teacher and identified with both the Lion and the Lamb. Events in the story can also be traced to Osiris of Egypt, Tammuz of Syria, Krishna (Christna) of India (dated 1,400 B.C.E.), and at least 28 other ancient Godmen. Mithras of Roman religion is particularly troubling for Christianity, because it assumes an Apocalypse, Judgment Day, Resurrection in the flesh, and a second coming of Mithras.

Most ancient civilizations had a godman mystery teaching. People knew the teachings were myths and not facts. The myths were developed over a period of many years to teach approved initiates the mysteries of how to be better people. They are great stories: stories of ancient ancestors struggling to learn how to live together in harmonious relationships.

Reading *The Greatest Story Ever Told* may create personal problems for other Christians similar to my reactions. For sometime, the research resulted in a mental-state of denial. I kept telling myself it couldn't possibly be true, or that my research must be faulty. The problem was that I did not want to believe the historical facts that scholars have known for many years. Also, it never entered my brain that such a voluminous quantity of biblical and non-biblical scholarly work exists on the subject of Divine Truth.

Christ Within!
(Christianity)

The search for Truth led to the study of writings attributed to Paul in the New Testament. To study what is actually written and not glossed-over by theologians quoting what Paul supposedly wrote. There are Biblical scholars and theologians that believe Paul's mission was to develop an acceptable godman type mystery teaching for the Jewish people that would compete with all of the other popular ancient mysteries at that time. Judaism was at a disadvantage because they did not have a mythical godman type story from the ancient mysteries.

Paul's stories had to compete by being equal to, or improve upon, all of the claims made for the others in the Mediterranean region. Creating a Jewish-based mystery would only be acceptable to the Jews if based upon stories in the Torah. That proved not to be a problem for Paul, because the name Joshua in the book of Exodus translates to Jesus in Greek. The Old Testament uses Joshua and the New Testament uses Jesus, which are identical depending on whether you are using the Hebrew or Greek language. By putting the mythical Torah stories of Joshua in Exodus into a modernized version, Paul created the Jesus mythical godman story for the Jews. There are scholars that believe Paul was successful far beyond anything that could have been predicted.

In the book *Jesus and the Lost Goddess*[1], pages 14-16, the authors state "Jewish Gnostics, and Christian Gnostics after them, understood Exodus to be an initiation allegory. Egypt represents the body. Whilst initiates identify with the body, they are 'in captivity.' To 'come forth out of Egypt' was understood as leaving behind the idea of being merely a body and discovering the soul. The ignorant Egyptians represent those 'without Gnosis,' who remain identified with their physical selves."

"Crossing the Red Sea was understood as symbolizing a purifying baptism, which is the first stage of initiation on the path to spiritual awakening for those who are 'conscious.' Paul writes: *"Our ancestors passed through the Red Sea and so received baptism into the fellowship of Moses."*[2]"

"The next step of initiation is about 'death' of the old self, represented by the death of Moses. Moses is mythically reborn as Joshua/Jesus who completes the journey to the Promised Land, representing the 'reborn' initiate who realizes Gnosis. The first stage of initiation is one of purification and

---

[1] *Jesus and the Lost Goddess*, Freke & Gandy, 2001 Harmony Books, NY, NY
[2] First Corinthians 10:1-6

struggle. In Exodus this is crossing the Red Sea, which inaugurates 40 years of wandering in the wilderness. In the Jesus story, this stage is represented by Jesus' baptism, followed by his 40 days in the wilderness. The next stage in the process of initiation is the 'death' of the old self, which precipitates Gnosis.[1] It is represented in the Exodus myth by the death of Moses and in the Jesus myth by the death of Jesus on the cross. The experience of Gnosis is represented in Exodus by Jesus (Joshua) crossing to the Promised Land and in the New Testament by Jesus' resurrection from the dead and ascension to Heaven."

Original Christians acknowledged their debt to Exodus by classifying people as 'the captive, the called, and the chosen.' Those Jews yet trapped in a physical body are like the Jews captive in Egypt. Those who have heard the call to awaken and begin the spiritual journey by being initiated into the outer mysteries of Christianity are like the Jews 'called out of Egypt' to begin the journey to their true home. Those who have undergone the process of purification and spiritual struggle necessary to prepare themselves for Gnosis and been chosen to be initiated into the secret inner mysteries of Christianity are like the 'chosen people' whom Jesus (Joshua) leads across the river Jordan to the Promised Land. Initiates who finally realized Gnosis were known as 'those who crossed over.' In Exodus 12 men were chosen to represent the 12 tribes of Israel. After baptism, Jesus likewise selects 12 men as his immediate followers. Such a reference is not surprising. Both motifs refer to the 12 astrological signs of the zodiac. Jews adopted astrology from the Babylonians while in exile and became renowned throughout the ancient world as astrologers."

The outstanding growth of Paul's Jewish mystery teaching occurred after Constantine proclaimed the state religion of the Roman Empire to be Christianity. The Roman authoritarian state religion developed into the Roman Catholic Church, as we know it today. Christianity experienced geometric growth by also incorporating the Mithras mysteries of Rome into Christianity. The Vatican is even built on top of a former Mithras shrine. Whatever the truth may be it was certainly a win/win situation for Constantine, the Roman Empire, and Christianity. The genius of the action was that former devoted Mithras participants merely changed the name of their religion from Mithraism to Christianity. The name was not important just as long as the dogma and creeds remained intact. Later, Pope Leo X (1475-1521) is quoted as saying: *the myth of Christ has served us well.*[2]

---

[1] Gnosis is an esoteric form of knowledge

[2] *The Messianic Legacy*, Page 2, Baigent, Leigh, Lincoln 1986 Dell Publishing

Why did it take 300 years for the church fathers to decide if Jesus was a mortal prophet or a God? Apparently no one thought it was of any importance prior to that time in history, and obviously many did not believe it to be true. The reason is twofold:

1. Constantine, the Roman ruler, needed to amalgamate all of the ancient mystery teachings, including Christianity, into one state religion for the Roman Empire. The growth of various mystery religions in the Roman Empire had created a major problem for the Emperor. A means was needed to manage the masses other than by the sword. Constantine used Christianity only as a means to achieve what he wanted. It was not his religion. In spite of church teachings, history confirms that Constantine did not convert from the pagan religion of Sol Invictus. He purposely deferred baptism until his dying moment in 335 C.E., at age 64 in the baths of Aquyrion, hoping that he would be cleansed of his sins as Christianity taught. Constantine had killed his second wife Fausta, his son Crispus, and his nephew Licinianus, in addition to thousands of innocent people to achieve his personal desires. His son Crispus had rendered his father invaluable aid as an experienced soldier in the campaign against Licinus. In 326 C.E. he was executed by orders from his father Constantine, who was a ruthless ruler and not a Christian.[1]

2. The leaders of Christianity had an opportunity for their teachings to become the state religion of the Roman Empire. Christians were previously treated severely. On May 20, 325 C.E. at the Nicene Convention they voted to determine if Jesus was a mortal prophet or a god. The voting resulted in only 218 for the motion that Jesus should from that day forward be known as a God. By voting that Jesus was a God assured Christian leaders of many converts from the other mystery teachings. The decision of only 218 men, all with a personal interest to protect, dictated to the world that Jesus would be known as a God. Consubstantiality won-out over Similarity that day.

The church and politics were one and the same at that time in history. Stretching the truth to achieve an advantage has always been acceptable in politics. Many bishops were against the proposal to vote for Jesus as a god. After much debate there were 17 holdouts that were later reduced to the final two that were exiled from the Roman Empire. The church destroyed all of exiled church leaders works.

---

[1] *Egypt, Greece and Rome, Civilizations of the Ancient Mediterranean*, By C. Freeman, Oxford Univ. 1996

Eusebius began his career as a scribe in the library and was later commissioned to write the imperial biography of Constantine. He wrote inspiring chapters about the Emperor's piety and wonderful works, and how Constantine governed his empire in a Christian manner for over thirty years.

Many scholars rate Eusebius as the greatest liar of all time. He also wrote about the Council of Nicaea, which his emperor Constantine had convened and chaired the meeting of church bishops. The Council was so important to Constantine that he provided the funds for all of their expenses. Constantine opened the meeting with a plea to restore the unity of the church, which was severely divided on the issue of the divinity of Jesus.

Arius, a priest from Baucalis, Egypt along with many other bishops and priests had been teaching that Christ was not one with God, but a created figure. The doctrines were the continuity of Platonic ideas that came through the Stoics, Philo, Plotinus, Origen, etc., which had deeply influenced Christian theology. Those doctrines were now in conflict with Christianity. In his writings about the Council, Eusebius conveniently omits any reference to Arius or the sharply divided bishops that were coerced into voting with the majority. Arianism teaches similarity of Jesus to God and rejects consubstantiality, which teaches God and Jesus are one and the same.

The question of consubstantiality rather than similarity of the Son and Father was absolutely vital politically, and to the developing theology of Christianity. If priests and bishops taught that Christ was not God, which many believed, then the value of the Christian church to the Emperor Constantine and the state would be rendered useless. Also, it could create chaos by destroying the unity and authority of the church. Athanasius, an eloquent archdeacon under Alexander, argued that if Christ and the Holy Spirit were not one with the Father then polytheism would prevail. He admitted that it is difficult to vision three persons in one God, but reason must concede to the mystery of the Trinity. The Council developed the following creed with Constantine's approval:

"We believe in one God, the Father Almighty, maker of all things visible or invisible; and in one Lord Jesus Christ, the Son of God, begotten...not made, being of one essence with the Father...who for us men and our salvation came down and was made flesh, was made man, suffered, rose again the third day, ascended into heaven, and comes to judge the quick and the dead." [1,2]

---

[1] *Cambridge Medieval History*, I, 121
[2] Revised to the Nicene Creed in 362 C.E.

Constantine was so elated with the decision that he hosted a royal dinner for those present at the Nicaea Council. He also issued an imperial edict that all books by Arius and others not supporting the Creed were to be burned, and concealment of any such books to be punishable by death. The Emperor exiled from the Roman Empire those not signing the Creed. The unanimity of the Creed gave the medieval Church the name of Catholic. This action replaced paganism with Christianity as the religion of the Roman Empire and gave Constantine absolute control. Christianity was then adopted as the state religion of the Roman Empire.

Christianity did not destroy paganism; it adopted it. The Greek language reigned for centuries over philosophy, which became the vehicle of the Christian literature and ritual. The Greek mysteries passed down into the impressive mystery of the Mass. Other pagan cultures contributed to the syncretistic result. From Egypt came the idea of a divine trinity, the last judgment, and a personal immortality of reward and punishment, and the adoration of the Mother and Child.[1] From Phrygia came the worship of the Great Mother; from Syria the resurrection drama of Adonis; from Thrace the cult of Dionysus the dying and saving god. From Persia came millenarianism, the "ages of the world," the final conflagration, the dualism of Satan and God, of Darkness and Light. The more ancient Mithraic ritual so closely resembled the Eucharistic sacrifice of the Mass that Christian fathers charged the Devil with inventing these similarities prior to Christianity to mislead frail minds. Christianity was the last great creation of the ancient pagan world.[2]

From the pagan teachings, Christianity offered mankind a very attractive religion. It was offered without any restrictions to all humans, classes, and to all countries. It was not limited to one ethnic group like Judaism. Slaves and freemen alike could become the recipients of the teaching of Christ's victory over death. The church matured by inheriting and accepting the responsibilities of the Roman Empire as it died in giving birth to Christianity. Paul had been the tireless theologian several hundred years earlier in developing the doctrine of Christ. Now his teachings could be openly taught during the medieval age. He had transformed the Jesus of the Greek gospels into the Christ of theology. Among his many works, Paul wrote perhaps the greatest words about love that have ever been written, which we read in First Corinthians, Chapter 13: Verses 1-13 the following:

"If I speak in the tongues of men and of angels, but have not love, I am a noisy gong or a clanging cymbal. And if I have prophetic powers, and

---

[1] See page 113, Hieroglyphic quote from *Egyptian Book of the Dead*, *"Thus being one god I became three."*
[2] *The Story of Civilization*, (10 Volumes) Will Durant, Vol. 2, pg.595

understand all mysteries and all knowledge, and if I have all faith, so as to remove mountains, but have not love, I am nothing. If I give away all I have, and if I deliver my body to be burned, but have not love, I gain nothing.

"Love is patient and kind; love is not jealous or boastful; it is not arrogant or rude. Love does not insist on its own way; it is not irritable or resentful; it does not rejoice at wrong, but rejoices in the right. Love bears all things, believes all things, hopes all things, and endures all things.

"When I was a child, I spoke like a child, I reasoned like a child; when I became a man, I gave up childish ways. For now we see in a mirror dimly, but then face to face. Now I know in part; then I shall understand fully, even as I have been fully understood. So Faith, Hope, Love abide, these three; but the greatest of these is Love."[1]

While studying the writings of Paul one verse took me totally by surprise when he wrote, *"To them God chose to make known how great among the Gentiles are the riches of the glory of this **mystery, which is Christ in you**, the hope of glory."[2]* That is a mystery teaching and the secret of Christianity. The statement has nothing to do with a historical Jesus. Paul also wrote from the ancient mystery teachings: *"The unspiritual (non-initiated) man does not receive the gifts of the spirit of God, for they are folly to him, and he is not able to understand them because they are spiritually discerned. **The spiritual man judges all things, but is himself to be judged by no one.**"[3]* Paul is referring to the ancient mysteries and explaining the difference between the Inner Person (initiated or spiritual) and the Outer Person (non-initiated).

There can be no other meaning from the positive statement of Paul, *"the spiritual man judges all things, but is himself to be judged by no one."* Why do preachers and the church avoid that type of scripture? Paul is developing the theology of how important it is for each individual to discover the Christ that exists within each one of us. It has nothing to do with the mystery of Jesus. Why does Christianity not teach us how to become spiritual people, instead of how to be faithful followers of a father type image? Did you ever hear a preacher say that a spiritual person judges all things, but is himself to be judged by no one? Have you ever heard a sermon on how important it is to discover that Christ is actually within you? Do they teach that it is your personal responsibility to discover the Christ that dwells within, rather than have blind-faith and attempt to be a duplicate copy of Jesus?

Might ordained seminarians believe that only people who have studied theology in a seminary can truly become a spiritual person? With all

---

[1] *Holy Bible*, Revised Standard Version 1946-1952
[2] Colossians 1: verse 27
[3] 1 Corinthians 2: verses 14-15

of the pomp, pageantry, and vestments worn in many churches today it appears they want to impress the congregation about something they believe that sets them apart from the congregation. To many laypersons it appears as sanctimonious action. After all, theology in a seminary is nothing more than to study, and later justify to others, whatever the religious institution believes and teaches.

It is now obvious that Pastor Cyrus Moorhead was telling me exactly what Paul meant when he said, *"Someday you will learn that **Christ is within you.**"* Paul wrote, ***"Christ in you,"*** and prefaced it by saying, *"the riches of the glory of this mystery."* That is the mystery of Christianity.

Since a Christ can be anyone, it now makes me very suspicious that Pastor Moorhead fully understood that his ministry actually came from the teachings of the *ancient mysteries.* For what other reason would he say that someday you will learn that Christ is within you? As stated earlier, Pastor Cyrus Moorhead never used the name of Jesus in the woodshop. He was expected to, but never did. Why? If only he were alive to explain the reason. Perhaps Cy was not completely comfortable with the Presbyterian theology and thought that someday his woodworking sinner friend would figure it all out for himself. Is that what Paul meant by saying the mystery of Christianity is Christ in you? Did he mean that you can get help, but you must personally solve the mystery?

Christianity developed from the teachings of Paul. His writings should be at the beginning of the New Testament, not following the first four Gospels. There is probably not a Biblical scholar alive that would disagree that Paul's writings pre-dated all of the other writings in the New Testament. Scholars also know that other New Testament writers used Paul's writings for reference. Also, why would the Nicene Council establish the order of Paul's writings to follow the others? Probably it was because there are mythical stories in the first four Gospels that were added to Paul's writing from the more ancient mysteries. The church fathers may have wanted to impress people early in the book with mythical stories like the virgin birth. The virgin birth and a physical resurrection were later additions to the story of Jesus. Even Paul and John do not refer to the birth of Jesus, although John does state that Jesus is the 'son of Joseph.'[1] It appears that John believed Jesus had a natural birth with human parents.

Christian theology has confused people by using the word Christ as synonymous with the name Jesus. When people use the name Christ it is never questioned and understood they mean Jesus. That is precisely what I

---

[1] John 1:45 and John 6:42

also believed, because it is what they taught me in Sunday school as a little boy. To fully understand the true meaning of the word Christ in a Biblical derivation, then Jesus may have been a Christ, but you can also be a Christ!

Khristos is a Greek translation of the Hebrew verb 'mashakh' meaning to anoint. In English it became Christ. In ancient Judaism it was a common occurrence to anoint people and refer to them as a 'mashakh person.' All it did was give them a title to differentiate the person from others, such as a supervisor or town official. Kings were also anointed and referred to as messiahs. The Jews understood the messiah to be a human leader, not something supernatural or a human extension of God. Jews have one and only one God. The use of the word Christ is similar to the word Lord. We know from Judaism that the father of an ancient family was a Lord. If kids got a spanking they would probably tell mommy, *our lord is mean.* Today they would say, *our daddy is mean,* or *my father is mean.* When people refer to the Lord and mean God or Jesus it is confusing. In the British Empire the word means a man of high rank that can participate in the House of Lords.

The church fails to teach that items like the virgin birth and physical body resurrection of Jesus were not a part of original Christianity. They were not added to Christianity until much later, in at least the ninth decade.[1] The divine nature of Jesus as the incarnation of a theistic God was also added later. Theism is the belief in a personal God that is creator and ruler of the world. Why should the decision of men only over 1,600 years ago dictate to the world who is, or is not, a God?

From that day in May 325 C.E. at the Council of Nicaea until the present, theologians have been at work attempting to justify the voting majority of 218 men. Thousands of people have been employed to develop the theology to support their decision. It was extremely troubling to learn that it took 300 years for Jesus to be voted a God, and the male-only vote was not unanimous. The truth of that issue would make a fascinating sermon. What additional knowledge could those church fathers have that voted no? It was a personal advantage to them for Jesus to be verified as God. One can't even imagine the courage it took for them to vote no on such an important issue.

Theology, dogma, and creeds are nothing more than human explanations attempting to justify the position those institutional religious organizations teach about what they claim to be true. Is it any wonder there are thousands of institutional religions all claiming, under the guise of divine inspiration, that their dogma and creed is the only true Word of God? They

---

[1] *The Life of Jesus Critically Reviewed*, Strauss, D.F., London 1973

may want the populace to believe their theology and dogma are divinely inspired, but the fact remains humans wrote every word, and continue to do so. Many of them cannot even make up their minds if women are capable to be ministers in Christianity. With the variety of religious institutions they are like super-markets; just shop around until you find something that fits your fancy.

To finally learn and understand that the true Christ can be within any person was a shocking revelation. Whether Christ is defined to mean truth, knowledge, knowing yourself, or something else; it does mean that many of us have been searching in the wrong places. Ancient theology does not teach that we must faithfully attend church every Sunday to find the Christ within. Paul found his 'Christ within' while traveling alone on a lonesome road to Damascus. It is now crystal clear that each person has the sole responsibility to find the esoteric truth that exists within. To do that, our personal Mission must be to 'Know Yourself' through commitments of the following type:

- To find the God of my being and of all things.
- To become aware of my divinity without rejecting my humanity.
- Seek Truth at all times and the Truth in all things.
- Learn who I am and the mystery of my consciousness.
- Deny my separate self and start communing with the Oneness of God.
- Develop an ego-less state of awareness.
- Forfeit the thoughts of a mortal body to discover immortal identity.
- Follow my heart not the herd.
- Practice the only commandment given by Jesus; *Love one another.*[1]

In the ancient town of Delphi in central Greece near Mt. Parnassus there was a famous temple that had the words **'Know Thyself'** carved in stone above the entrance. Plato writes, "it was put there for a salutation for all who enter the temple. Know thyself and be temperate are the same thing, yet they may be thought to be different. Self-knowledge is the very essence of temperance. Succeeding sages thought it was a piece of advice, not a salutation from the god as people entered, and they never added too much."[2]

Only a person that has the courage to take that lonesome and spiritual mental journey within their soul will ultimately learn the elusive Truth they have been seeking has always been within their body. Languishing in the comfort of a paternalistic type religion does not challenge the individual to

---

[1] John 13:34 (*A new commandment I give to you, that you should 'love one another.'*)
[2] *Charmides*, 164d,e

discover the esoteric Truth that exists within. We must personally find our individual divinity, and not mentally depend on some mystical father-type image to take care of us. That is resorting to theism; a daddy that will always look after us.

The euphoria of attending a church service soon abates for many of us as people return to the real world where they must live and conduct their life in the harsh realities of daily life and work. It is uplifting to attend a church service. The organ music, singing, an inspiring sermon, children performing, and beautiful surroundings are all pleasurable while participating. However, the question is, what do you actually take away that will inspire you all week during the highs and lows of a secular life? Test yourself. Can you honestly say that by Wednesday you remember the title of the sermon last Sunday?

Finally, it is now understandable that it was not humanly possible for that boy at the church altar in 1933 to have a 'Jesus Experience' through Pastor Charles McCaskey and his wife repeatedly telling him *"Hurry Up Son. You are delaying the church service. The others professed they found Jesus tonight and have gone back to their seats."*

What the other children were expressing was their euphoria of the moment. With parents and the congregation of the church present it was very tempting to agree with the preacher and say that you did have a Jesus experience and felt the warmth of His presence.

As ministers of a Christian church, the McCaskeys should have been teaching that eleven-year-old boy, at the church altar in 1933, how to learn what all of the *ancient mysteries* taught, including what Paul later wrote, *"the glory of this mystery, which is Christ in you."* That boy would have then learned how to discover the *'mystery of Christianity.'*[1] By teaching that curriculum, he would have learned that personal and honest introspection is the only way to discover individual spirituality: the Divine Truth that is within the soul of every human being. However, he should have been warned that the Divine Truth within every soul is very elusive!

It now seems certain that is what the McCaskeys were attempting to do. However, they confused us by calling it a 'Jesus Experience,' which inferred you should seek an external Godman, rather than teach us how to discover:

Christ is within you!

---

[1] See page 96

Sinners to Saviors

"*Millions of innocent men, women, and children, since the introduction of Christianity, have been burnt, tortured, fined, imprisoned; yet we have not advanced one inch towards uniformity. What has been the effect of the coercion? To make one half of the world fools, and the other half hypocrites. To support error and roguery all over the earth.*" – Thomas Jefferson, third president of the United States, and chairman of the five-man committee to draft the Declaration of Independence.

America's first presidents understood that the Puritan Protestant clerics would kill people or use any sadistic means they desired to enforce their Christian beliefs. The only way the Church could be prevented from continuing their human atrocities and sadistic acts was to fight for civil laws in the new country. Our presidents were fully aware of what Christianity was capable of doing to people without civil laws, when the Church was the self-appointed guardian of all sacred and secular matters. From the Nicene Convention to American Independence gave posterity a sickening legacy of 1,451 years of inhuman atrocities committed in the name of Christianity. Christian clerics were inventive geniuses to develop the devices used for torture. Even the ovens used by Nazi Germany in WWII were originally an invention of Christian clerics. The only difference was that the clerics rubbed their victims with lard so they would roast more thoroughly while still alive.[1]

Christianity, as we know it today, is the direct result of the Roman Emperor Constantine demanding that all religions be consolidated into one state religion for his personal benefit–a syncretic religion. The uniqueness of Christianity is that Pagan religions survived by being adopted into Christianity. Bishops were all too willing to negotiate Christianity into the position of being the Roman state religion at the Nicene Convention. The religion those bishops represented had already been appropriated from the *Ancient Mysteries,* with a change in name only. The bishops achieved their goal by voting Jesus a God, adopting the Easter Rule, developing the Nicene Creed (Apostles), and included spiritual teachings from the ancient mysteries. To further strengthen the position for Christianity, the bishops declared that everything they had appropriated from the *Ancient Mysteries* were revelations received from God as His True Word, and was now the 'gospel truth.' Will Durant wrote in the classic ten-volume history, *The Story of Civilization,* "Christianity was the last great creation of the ancient pagan world."

---

[1] *The Dark Side of Christianity*, by Helen Ellerbe, Morningstar & Lark, Orlando FL 1999

Constantine gave the bishops the right to enforce Christianity by any means they desired. That decree gave the Church absolute control and the self-appointed rights to be the guardian and definer of all sacred and secular matters. Truth was restricted to what Christianity declared it to be. All other religious competition was eliminated within the Roman Empire. Previous beliefs that brought initiates into intimate contact with the divine reality of God were classed heretical, absolutely forbidden, and punishable by death. Spoken or written words that may lead people to discover truth, spirituality, or science of any kind was also punished by torture and death. Education other than by the Church was eliminated. The horrible Dark Ages, Inquisitions, atrocities of the Medieval Age, and hundreds of years of witch-hunts were all the direct result of forcing Christianity upon the masses. The torture chamber was a legal option, except in America, until the Vatican wrote the *Codex Juris Canonici* in 1917.

Protestant preachers have insisted that only Catholics committed the many years of atrocities and sadistic acts in the name of God and the Church. Apparently their seminaries never taught them about people like John Calvin whose doctrine formed Presbyterianism had a powerful repressive police-state theocracy in Geneva, Switzerland. Calvin had a well known physician named Michael Servetus burned at the stake, because of his dissenting opinions about Christianity. John Knox, Calvin's pupil, violently condemned all other church creeds. A young nineteen-year-old Christian seminary student was hung in Scotland after other students reported that he had smiled while discussing the divinity of Jesus. There were Puritan laws in New England that decreed the death penalty for children who might curse or "smite" their parents. In today's newspapers we read about parents that may wish the New England law was still in effect to get rid of obnoxious kids, rather than the parents now serving time in prison.

The Church teaches that an understanding of past events will help to guide us in the future. What they generally mean is if they teach only the 'good stuff.' When people join a church they naturally assume it is the embodiment of pureness and sacredness. Christianity could have more influence if they would explain to people about the past history and how misled clerics committed such horrible sins. By explaining how Christianity 'cleaned-up its act' could be a powerfully impressive role model for all of we sinners to follow. Christianity is a classic example of *'sinners to saviors.'*

A person betrothed to marry a converted whore and a murderer, or a rapist and a murderer, should be fully apprised of their previous major sins. Humans respect and admire converted sinners that are open and honest about their past problems, and use that bad experience as a role model to teach others what they should avoid. Many people would feel more positive about their Christian heritage if the *'converted bride'* (Church) would teach communicant classes about her past problems and sins before requiring prospective members to say, *"I do – believe."* Of course, that will probably not be done because all denominations believe they are the *'epitome of piety'* and teach tyro preachers accordingly, which Thomas Jefferson called hypocrisy. To Learn about the former evil side of Christianity on your own initiative is extremely disappointing for anyone that has revered the teachings, and supposed purity, of the Christian church since they were little children.

Christianity, however, should not be outright rejected due to past problems and sins caused by an excess of power and authority. There were many Christians that fought against the tyranny of the Church, and preached love and forgiveness rather than fear and punishment. The Church put many of those pious people to death. Christianity does teach wisdom that has evolved from the *Ancient Mysteries*. By teaching that wisdom and functioning under civil law, Christianity has become a very positive religion. Christianity can lead people to discover their spirituality, but it should refrain from trying to dominate and control human freedom and spirituality.

A Christian church is also an excellent institution to protect people with frail minds–people that must be told what they should believe, and take comfort in a paternalistic-type religion. Pastors excel at doing both. That approach creates employment for thousands of people worldwide who are employed by many different religious institutions. It does not, however, place the responsibility where it belongs. Research has convinced me that a person who is genuinely seeking Divine Truth has the sole responsibility to make that discovery within his or her body (soul). Paul called it the, *mystery, which is Christ in you.* That reference to Christ does not mean Jesus.

Christianity has no restrictions to all humans, classes, and countries. It is not limited to any ethnic group. It is even tolerant with people that are not Bible literalists; people who challenge Christian theology; people who believe all Biblical myths and fantasies were composed by common men, not prophets as the Church claims; people who believe the Bible cannot be the True Word of God due to so many conflicting stories; and people that know the Bible has errors of science, which even the Church admits.

I have associated with only two pastors in my life that could be called magnanimous–pastors that have the patience and empathy to tolerate questions that may appear to differ with their beliefs about the foundation of Christianity and its theology. Questions that are asked with a genuine desire to learn, and not be rebuked by saying this is a Faith-based religion and questions are out of order. Cy Moorhead imparted wisdom and would discuss

Christian theology that conveyed confidence and sincerity. Cy obviously understood that his woodworking sinner friend could be difficult for a pastor. In his humble manner, he gave me hope that Divine Truth could be discovered through continued affiliation with Christianity.

Many years later, I found Dr. R. Leslie Holmes. Leslie is a pastor that compassionately understands individuals that are honestly and diligently still searching for Divine Truth late in their life. He worked in a department store in Belfast, Ireland and took welding classes to qualify for the United States quota system. When he arrived in the United States in 1967 with a wife and small son the immigration officer asked, "why are you coming to this country?" He answered, "to make a million."

Welding jobs were not available so he took a job in retail business. Later, Leslie heard his Uncle Sam Heslip, a gospel minister, explain what he refers to as "the link of grace." *"The day after I had learned about grace, it seemed so unbelievably wonderful that I was sure I had misunderstood him, so I went back to question him further. Four days later, I knew I wanted to spend the rest of my life telling people what I had just learned. I'm amazed at how far grace can go with a wee boy from Belfast. It really is, amazing."*[1]

The transition from Ireland to America, then many years later to an earned doctorate and pastor in Pittsburgh, Pennsylvania, all with a growing family was extremely difficult. Those difficult years molded him into a pastor with empathy and the ability to understand people that are a genuine problem, and a nuisance for many pastors. During lunch one day, Dr. Holmes was given a copy of my funeral arrangements, which I had prepared. I told him it was my firm belief that funerals should be a happy affair and celebrate the life of the deceased, or just celebrate that you are finally rid of the old goat. His reaction to my questions and statements confirmed that I had finally found another pastor with many of the characteristics written about Jesus. Everyone should be so fortunate as to find a pastor, rabbi, or priest with those attributes.

Sigmund Freud was the father of psychoanalytic discipline who wrote the book, *The Future of an Illusion.* In the book he argues that, *"Religion was a major human creation. Religion was a coping mechanism for the human response to the trauma of self-consciousness, to keep hysteria under control, and to manage for self-conscious creatures the shock of existence."* Freud believed that he had discovered in religion the manifestation of trauma, not the manifestation of truth. Freud may or may not be correct; however, Christianity is an ideal coping mechanism to manage the trauma of human self-consciousness, and be a security system for human life. A magnanimous

---

[1] *LIFE TIMES the Christian Magazine for Northern Ireland*, Belfast, Ireland, February 2002

pastor is a great asset for laymen raised in Christianity to teach us how to discover the coping mechanism and security system we all need in our lives.

We live in a violent galaxy where our earth could be disintegrated instantaneously. By following the teachings attributed to Jesus, the most profound wisdom of mankind, you would be prepared for any apocalyptic event and your instant demise. What He stands for is the foundation of Christianity. People that cannot accept the divinity of Jesus are urged to follow His teachings, rather than be devoid of spiritual convictions. Christianity taught by St. Paul offers what mankind has always, and always will seek, which is to discover the *'truth within your soul'* – Divine Truth.

Searching for Divine Truth must go beyond, and much deeper than, what others may claim to be the True Word of God. Every religion that believes in the existence of a Supreme Being will contain truths that can lead you to discover that God is the author of everything that exists; the Eternal, the Supreme, the Living, and Awful Being; from whom nothing in the universe is hidden. Theologians from all religions may try to convince you their institutional beliefs were received directly as the True Word of God. Your personal efforts will ultimately lead you to discover Divine Truth, *as you understand it*, and not what others might claim it to be.

The search for Divine Truth has confirmed that Christianity will remain the choice of all religious institutions to help fulfill my peculiar needs. Since Christianity has evolved from being controlled by misled clerics for so many years, to a true savior-type religion, it is an excellent choice for all sinners or non-believers to seriously consider. As a syncretistic religion, Christianity includes, and teaches, wisdom from the *Hebrew Scriptures, Ancient Mysteries*, and the *Egyptian Ma'at*. Studying wisdom from those ancient sources will teach important lessons while searching for Divine Truth.

A landmark day in the quest for Divine Truth is the day we finally understand why the preposition *'in'* must be removed from *'Believe in God'* (theism)–that is the day we start learning how to *'**Believe God**!'*

May you be successful in the search for Divine Truth.

****

Perhaps humanity is arriving at an era in the evolution of religion when all of God's people, including theologians, acknowledge that any language invented by humans introduces constraints and misinterpretations that make it impossible to define God in human terms. We should recognize that no organized religious institution has ever changed the ancient Egyptian teachings that were written in hieroglyphics thousands of years before men created all other religions: *"God is hidden and no man knoweth his form. God is a mystery unto all creatures."*

Postscript

The following announcement was too important not to include in this book, although pre-printing work was nearly completed.

Boston, MA, August 12, 2002.
<u>Jews can be saved without faith in Jesus!</u>

The Organization representing U. S. Catholic bishops announced today that after spending hundreds of years trying to convert Jews to Christianity, that it is now theologically unacceptable to target Jews for evangelization. The United States Conference of Catholic Bishops declared unequivocally that the Biblical covenant between Jews and God is valid and therefore Jews do not need to be saved through faith in Jesus.

In case they missed the above announcement, my Jewish friends will be pleased to learn they can now be saved without faith in Jesus, or converting to Christianity–if they considered it to be a problem! It is good news to learn we may now see our Jewish friends in the hereafter, unless, of course, Christian theology doesn't change again.

The above announcement is a profound theological decision, which some Protestant denominations have also been debating. It will further confuse Christian laypeople. We have been taught *unequivocally* that salvation is only possible through faith in Jesus. Theologians have been questioned, *what happens to non-believers?* Never did I get an answer from theologians or 'so-called' Christian experts other than, *the only possible way a person can be saved is through faith in Jesus.* Preachers have told me that '*salvation through faith in Jesus'* is fundamental to Christianity and can never be questioned.

The Nicene Convention was held 1,677 years ago. To learn that Church bishops are still trying to decide what the truth is about Jesus will be very disconcerting to Protestants believers. It will be fascinating to learn what the Protestant theologians will now decide.

Bibliography

Books and Reading Suggestions

Searching for Divine Truth should be an enjoyable lifetime learning experience. There are thousands of books by good research scholars that may be of help to you. Also, the Internet is a good source of information. The books listed are not classed as theological books. Theology is a system or school of opinions concerning God and religious questions, or a course of specialized religious study at a college or university. Seminaries are religious institutions that teach what that particular institution claims to be true. If they believe the moon is made of green cheese then students will be taught how to justify and teach that belief to others. (Refer to pages 98-99)

Books listed on the following pages are excellent reading material. They are not listed in any specific order of importance. When you are studying any book or document that is fascinating and contributing to your knowledge then that is the most important one at that particular time. During the past several years each of these books have been read and studied. Some are so fascinating and controversial they have been read several times. At least twelve of them have been written in the past five years from sources of research material that was not previously available.

There may be items in the text that have not been correctly cross-referenced or proper credit given to the author of the original source of material. If that has occurred then my apologies are extended to the author whose book is referred to in the bibliography.

Hurry Up Son was never intended to be a scholarly achievement. The subjects written about would have been presented in a different manner if the original intent had been to reach a larger audience than just the author's family and friends. This book was written as an honest and truthful effort to document items from the author's life and things he has learned from personal research. My only desire was to help family and friends in their search for Divine Truth. There is a vast source of scholarly material now available that directly conflicts with what the author was taught to believe, which started when he was a young boy.

Egypt, Greece and Rome, Civilizations of the Ancient Mediterranean, by Charles Freeman, Oxford University Press, 1996, approx. 600 pages. The author comes from a long line of classical scholars and writers. The research and reading suggestions in this book certainly ranks it as a great work of history. It covers the time period of Egypt, 3200 B.C., through the Byzantine Empire in the 6th Century. The author's attempt was, *to create a single volume overview, which may provide a springboard into further study of these fascinating societies.* He certainly achieved that in a very readable book.

Religion and Science, Historical and Contemporary Issues, by Ian G. Barbour, Harper Collins, 1997, 368 pages. The author is retired professor of physics and religion at Carleton College, Northfield, MN. The book won 1999 Templeton Prize for Progress in Religion. Nine chapters are from the Gifford Lectures in Scotland and published as *Religion in an Age of Science.* Professor Barbour writes in the book about "Nature Centered Spirituality," "Chaos Theory and Complexity," "God as Communicator of Information," "God as Determiner of Indeterminacies," and explores relevance of alternative views in relation to environmental ethics. Chapter 12 consisting of 27 pages titled "God and Nature" makes it well worth the price of the book.

The Bible as History, by Dr. Werner Keller, Bantam Books revised edition, 1982, paperback and 465 pages. The author is a German non-theologian journalist born in 1905. He covers an incredible 4,000-year adventure into the past to reveal the historical foundation of the Holy Bible and admits he has a special fascination with Biblical archeology. The book reads like an exciting detective story. Even agnostics should be pleased with the careful examination and results of scientific investigation.

Care Of The Soul, author Thomas Moore, Harper Collins publisher, 1994, paperback and 312 pages. The author was a Catholic monk for 12 years and is now a leading lecturer and writer in areas of archetypal psychology with degrees in music, psychology, and theology. He states in the Introduction that, *soul work is not an adjustment to any accepted norms. Rather, the goal is a richly elaborated life, connected to society and nature, woven into the culture of family, nation and globe. To be profoundly connected to ancestors and to living brothers and sisters in the many communities that claim our hearts. The human soul is not meant to be understood.* This would be a far more valuable handbook if the author had included an index. It gives good counseling on many items, but requires the reader to make notes for cross-reference and devise his own index.

Dead Sea Scrolls Deception, authors Michael Baigent and Richard Leigh, Simon & Schuster, 1993, paperback and 268 pages. Discovered in 1947, the Dead Sea Scrolls were kept a tight secret by the Roman Catholic Church because they challenge the Church's version of the facts. *Antiquity* (UK) states, *A racy tale of archaeological sins, religious bigotry, academic megalomania, misconduct and possible criminality.* The authors claim a *small enclave of biblical scholars painstakingly concealed information in the Dead Sea Scrolls about the connection between the elusive figure of James, Jesus' brother, whose dispute with Paul precipitated Christianity.* A fascinating book with a good Index and Bibliography

The Harlot By The Side Of The Road, Forbidden Tales of the Bible, by Jonathan Kirsch, Ballantine Books, 1997, paperback and 395 pages. The author is a writer, lawyer, and has degrees in Russian and Jewish history. If you believe the Bible is all Holy Writ then reading this book will give you the shock of your life. The author is a Bible student that regularly reads the Bible to his children. Like clerics have done for centuries, he censors what is read to children because he says, *it is just too "juicy."* Religious authorities throughout history have suppressed the Bibles shocking tales of sex, violence, and scandal. This book includes a Reader's Guide, an excellent Index, and Recommended Reading and Bibliography. In this book you will learn truths about what is in the Bible that no cleric would dare to preach from his pulpit, unless he wishes to be unemployed. As James Miles, author of *God: A Biography* states, *the Bible is written for adults, not for children, and some parts for adults only.*

VITRUVIUS, The Ten Books on Architecture, translated by Professor Morris H. Morgan of Harvard University, Dover Books, 1960, paperback and 331 pages. The ten books in the title are actually chapters that average only 30 pages per book. This little 5-inch by 8-inch book belongs in every curious minded and thinking person's library. Marcus Vitruvius Pollio lived in the first century B.C. He was an architect and engineer that wrote the most influential and oldest existing book on architecture. Even Michelangelo was a careful student of the writings of Vitruvius. Cathedrals and buildings all over the world reveal the major influence of Vitruvius. The fascination of this book to the non-architect is the wide variety of subjects covered, such as symmetry, harmony (music), proportion, acoustics, human body, materials, colors, durability and beauty to polished finishes, the moon, pumps, water organ, water clock, constellations, finding water, and many other ordinary everyday things. There are many drawings and sketches. The origin of the

Three Orders, Corinthian, Ionic, and Doric, including drawings is presented in simple language and knowledge that everyone should have. At a price of $10.95 this book is a valuable education at a very low price.

PLATO, The Collected Dialogs, including the Letters, edited by Edith Hamilton and Huntington Cairns, Princeton University Press, fourteenth printing November 1989, hardback and 1,743 pages with an excellent Introduction. Plato was born in 428 B.C. and died in 348 B.C. He was from a very ancient Greek family. Socrates was the teacher of Plato and Aristotle was Plato's student. Plato presented his ideas in the form of dramatic dialogues. As a philosopher, he was always searching for truth. Plato referred to God as the Ordering One. Early Christianity closely followed the teachings of Plato in the belief that Jesus was similar to God and not consubstantial. No human form could be equal to God in Platonic teachings. When Augustine of Hippo, a brilliant theologian, wrote and argued persuasively for consubstantiation and the trinity at the Nicene Convention, the established church adopted his theology. That action precipitated the main stream of Christianity to start parting ways with long-held Platonic philosophy within the Christian church. Some branches of Christianity have never accepted consubstantiate beliefs or the belief in a trinity.

The Nag Hammadi library, Editor James M. Robinson, Harper Collins, 1990, paperback and 550 pages. Do not confuse with the Dead Sea Scrolls. In December 1945 two farmer brothers, Muhammud and Khalifah Ali, found a sealed jar while searching for fertilizer in the hills of Upper Egypt near the town of Nag Hammadi. The jar contained thirteen ancient Coptic codices with some fifty texts. The discovery represented the most significant manuscript discovery of the twentieth century for the study of the New Testament and Christian origins, according to Trinity Press International. The jar contained the Gospel of Thomas, which played a crucial role in the newly emerging view of early Christianity as a very diverse phenomenon and in recent revival of studies of the historical Jesus.

The Fifth Gospel, The Gospel of Thomas Comes of Age, translated by Stephen Patterson, James Robinson, and Hans-Gebhard Bethge. Publisher Trinity Press International, 1998, paperback and 119 pages. From the Nag Hammadi discovery written in Coptic, a new way to write the tongue of Pharaonic Egypt, which was still in use when Christians first went to Egypt. This Gospel presents no story of Jesus, no accounts of his birth, life, death, or resurrection. It is a collection of 114 sayings ascribed to Jesus, each introduced with the simple formula, "Jesus says." About one-half of the sayings were already known as they appear in the canonical gospels. It tells no story of Jesus' life as embellished in the canonical gospels.

Page 37: *The sayings ascribed to Didymos Judas Thomas are a curious name. Only one part is a bona fide given name: Judas. Didymos is the Greek word for 'twin' and Thomas (Thoma) the Semitic word for twin. Could it be that the Gospel of Thomas intends to claim as its author Judas, the twin brother of Jesus?*

Page 53: *This basic idea—that Jesus is the redeemer come from God into a hostile and evil world to rescue a stranded race of chosen ones—is akin to ancient religious movement that found expression in the many different religions of the ancient orient, known as Gnosticism. When the redeemer comes and speaks a word of truth; the knowledge (gnosis) of who they really are, they remember, awaken from their slumber, and long once again to be reunited with the one true God.* These comments and others made by the translators are certainly fascinating to study.

Life Lines, by Dr. R. Leslie Holmes, Ambassador-Emerald, International, 2000, Hardback and 166 pages. Dr. Lloyd Ogilvie, Chaplain of the United States Senate says, *Leslie Holmes is one of America's finest pastors and scholar preachers.* This is an excellent book for your library. Thirty-seven of these books have been given to my family, friends, and business associates. Each of the eighteen chapters asks a question. The author's answers are based on non-controversial Christian theology for believers.

Why Christianity Must Change or Die, by John S. Spong, former Episcopal Bishop of Newark, NJ, Harper Collins 1999. This little 250-page paperback is listed after *Life Lines*, because it is a direct challenge to current Christian theology. The author retired in 2000 and is now a lecturer at Harvard University. You will learn things from reading this book that your preacher would probably prefer you did not know. He argues as to why the Apostle's Creed, Lord's Prayer, and other theology teachings are not applicable in today's technological age.

Jesus And The Lost Goddess, by T. Freke & P. Gandy, Harmony Books, New York, NY 2001. See page 91 for quote from this book.

The Inspiration And Authority Of The Bible, by B. B. Warfield, Presbyterian and Reformed Publishing House, Phillipsburg, NJ 1948.

Finding God At Harvard, K. Monroe Editor, Zondervan Publishing 1996.

The Case For Christ, by Lee Strobel, Zondervan Publishing, Grand Rapids, Michigan 1998.

Reclaiming The Dead Sea Scrolls, by L. H. Schiffman, Doubleday 1994.

ROSSLYN, Guardian Of The Secrets Of The Holy Grail, authors are Tim Murphy and Marilyn Hopkins, Element Books Limited, Boston, MA 2000.

The Templar Revelation, authors are L. Picknett & Clive Prince, Simon & Schuster Publisher, New York, NY 1998.

What Did Biblical Writers Know & When Did They Know It?, by W.G. Dever, W.B. Eerdman Publishing Company, Grand Rapids, Michigan 2001.

A Pilgrim's Path, by John J. Robinson, M. Evans & Company, New York, New York 1993.

Key To The Sacred Pattern, by H. Lincoln, St. Martins Press, New York, New York 1998.

The Dead Sea Scrolls Deception, by M. Baigent & R. Leigh, Simon & Schuster, New York, New York 1993.

Holy Blood Holy Grail, by M. Baigent, R. Leigh, and H. Lincoln, Dell Publishing, New York, NY 1982.

101 Myths Of The Bible, by G. Greenberg, Sourcebooks, Inc., Naperville, IL published in 2000.

Sacred Origins Of Profound Things, by C. Panati, Penguin Books, New York, NY 1996.

Born In Blood, by John J. Robinson, M. Evans & Co., New York, NY 1989.

The Secret Architecture Of Our Nations Capital, by D. Ovason, Harper Collins, New York, NY 1999.

The Dark Side of Christian History, by Helen Ellerbe, Morning Star & Lark, Orlando, FL 1999.

The Egyptian Book of the Dead, otherwise known as, ***The Book of the Great Awakening***, transliteration and translation by E. A. Wallis Budge, published 1895, reprint 1967 Dover Pub. 378 pages. This papyrus was found in perfect condition in 1888, and is 78 feet long by 15 inches wide. It is from the Theban period and was used among the Egyptians until the Christian era. Discovery of the Rosetta stone in 1799 on the Nile River delta made it possible to decipher Egyptian hieroglyphics.

As noted on page 95 of *Hurry Up Son*, Christianity is a syncretistic result from pagan cultures. For example, Christians are taught the Trinity, union of three divine persons, originated with Christianity. Following is how the Egyptian hieroglyphics quote their god, which was written nearly five thousand years before Christianity, *"I united myself to my shadow, and I sent forth Shu and Tefnut out of myself;* ***thus being one god I became three.*** *I, the evolver of evolutions evolved myself. No heaven existed, and no earth, and no terrestrial animals or reptiles had come into being. I formed them out of the mass of watery matter; I found no place to stand. I was alone; there existed none other who worked with me. I laid the foundations of all things by my will, and all things evolved themselves therefrom."*

Following is a condensed description of God given on pages xcii and xciii, *God is a spirit, a hidden spirit. God is from the beginning, and He hath been from the beginning.* ***God is hidden and no man knoweth his form. He is a mystery unto his creatures. God is Truth and He liveth by Truth and He feedeth thereon****. God is life and through Him only man liveth.* ***God is father and mother***, *the father of fathers, and the mother of mothers. He begetteth, but was never begotten; He produceth, but was never produced; He begat himself and produced himself. God made the universe, He is merciful unto those who reverence Him, and heareth him that calleth Him, rewardeth him that serveth Him, and He protecteth him that follow Him.*

For Egyptians to define God in the Ma'at philosophy of Truth as being the *mother of mothers and the father of fathers* is certainly different than the description given of God in the Old Testament. The Hebrew God, later Christian that we were taught to worship was meant to be feared. As children, we couldn't believe that even the meanest man in our town could be so vile as the patriarchal, murderous, and war loving God in the Old Testament stories.

The Power Of NOW, A Guide To Spiritual Enlightenment, by Eckhart Tolle, hardback 191 pages, New World Library, Novato, CA 1999. This book was received as a Father's Day gift from my grandson, Thomas V. Bonoma II, after the manuscript for *Hurry Up Son* was completed. This is an excellent book to learn techniques for achieving an uncluttered mind, to learn how to live in the present, not in the past or projected future. The book states that, *Christ is your God essence of self,* and on Page 96, *Do not turn your attention elsewhere in your search for TRUTH, for it is nowhere else to be found but within your body.*

INDEX

To

Hurry Up Son!

INDEX